ACCLAIM FOR SMOKY TRUDEAU

Front-Word, Back-Word, Insight Out is the Fiction Writer's Workshop Smoky taught at community colleges and other venues for eight years. Here are just a few of the nice things her students have said:

> *Smoky's impeccable writing expertise and teaching skills inspired me to write a short story that not only won a local competition but will soon be published in an anthology. That story will someday be a novel, and I owe it all to Smoky.*
>
> Sue Stewart

> *Your insights, energy, and sense of humor make you an outstanding teacher. You should win a prize.*
>
> Donald Sherbert, Ph.D.

> *Trudeau is a delight...she knows a lot and conveys examples in class tactfully and with skill.*

> *I always left class inspired...*
>
> Anonymous Student Evaluations

FRONT-WORD, BACK-WORD,

INSIGHT-OUT:

Lessons on Writing the Novel Lurking Inside You
From Start to Finish

by

Smoky Trudeau

Vanilla Heart Publishing

USA

FRONT-WORD, BACK-WORD, INSIGHT-OUT

Published by:

Vanilla Heart Publishing

www.vanillaheartbooksandauthors.com

10121 Evergreen Way, 25-156

Everett, WA 98204 USA

ISBN: 9780979654589

Library of Congress Control Number 2008927615

10 9 8 7 6 5 4 3 2 1 First Edition

First Printing, April 2008

Printed in the United States of America

Cover Design: Kimberlee Williams

FRONT-WORD, BACK-WORD,

INSIGHT-OUT:

Lessons on Writing the Novel Lurking Inside You
From Start to Finish

by

Smoky Trudeau

ACKNOWLEDGEMENTS

Thanks to all the students of the *Fiction Writer's Workshop* at Parkland Community College and Heartland Community College for making teaching such a pleasurable experience. Certain students in particular—Jack Houser, Sue Stewart, Don Sherbert, Melinda McIntosh, and others too numerous to name—made my job particularly rewarding.

A special thanks to Barbara Ardinger, Ph.D., for her help in compiling the Really Stupid Things Authors Do chapter, and Kathi Anderson for her support in all my writings.

Finally, thanks to Kimberlee Williams of Vanilla Heart Publishing for encouraging me to put my workshop in book form from which other aspiring writers can learn my methods.

DEDICATION

For my niece, Sarah, a talented writer in her own right, who I am honored to have touched and inspired. I love you, Sarah, and am very proud of you.

TABLE OF CONTENTS

FRONT-WORD

A few years back, while I was writing my first novel, *Redeeming Grace,* a workman came to my house to fix my dishwasher, which was leaking badly. I sat at the kitchen table, immersed in my writing, as he sat on the floor, immersed in finding the leak.

"You're sure typing fast," he said, looking up from the dismantled machine. "Whatcha in such a hurry for?"

I don't think he was trying to be nosey; but rather was just making small talk. So I answered him with the same good nature. "I'm writing a novel," I said.

His eyes lit up. "Oh!" he said. "I'm gonna write me a novel someday, maybe when I retire." He went back to his work.

I resisted the impulse to say, "And I'm going to take up dishwasher repair when *I* retire."

His response shouldn't have surprised me. According to one survey, more than 80 percent of Americans say they would like to write a book someday.[1] It's the literary version of the American dream.

The problem is, many of these aspiring authors have no idea how to make this literary dream a reality. They don't know any more about writing a book than I know about fixing dishwashers. And just as I wouldn't attempt to fix a dishwasher without going to trade school to learn, writers shouldn't attempt to write novels without first studying how it's done.

Oh sure, we all learn to write in school. We all learned how to state our thesis or story premise, give three or more supporting examples, then summarize. We did this whether we were writing a term paper or a short story. State your case. Give examples. Sum it up.

Do this when writing a novel and I can promise you: No publisher will get beyond the first page of your manuscript. As a former writing instructor, I can't tell you how many students come into my workshops and proceed to "set up" their stories, prattle on for page after page with boring prose that contains little setting description, no discernable plot, robotic characters, and boring dialogue, then summarize the entire story and call it an ending.

---

[1] *USA Today,* March 2005.

Writing a book is a commitment of time, a commitment of energy, a commitment of love. It's not unlike birthing and raising a child, and like raising a child, you want to get it right. Raise a child wrong and she is poorly prepared to make it in the real world. Write a book wrong and it will never make it into the publishing world.

Children don't come with instruction manuals. Fortunately, there is an instruction manual for writing a book. You're holding it in your hands. While I can't guarantee your book will be published, I can guarantee if you read this book and follow my suggestions, do the exercises provided, and diligently work on your writing every day, you'll be a much better writer afterward than you were beforehand.

CHAPTER ONE

GETTING STARTED

Where Do Stories Come From?

Since the dawn of humankind, stories have been used to teach, to entertain, and to enlighten. There seems to be a biological compulsion that makes people hungry to hear stories. There were more than 48,400 works of fiction published in 2007 in the United States alone, up from 28,400 only four years earlier.[1] But where do the writers of those books get their ideas? Where do stories come from?

When you're a writer, everything is research. Everything that happens to you, everything you see happening to others, is your raw material. Places you go, things you do, people you meet, all are the ingredients from which stories are created.

---

[1] Bowker's Books In Print Intellimarket

Stories are in the people you meet. I once met a woman who wrote copious amounts of very bad poetry in spiral notebooks. She carried those notebooks everywhere, hoping for an audience that would allow her to read her poetry aloud. She became the inspiration behind the main character in my story, *Good-bye, Emily Dickinson.*

Stories are in the places you visit. Hemingway wrote many, many stories based on his visits to Africa. Eudora Welty and Flannery O'Connor wrote stories set in their beloved South. The setting for my first novel, *Redeeming Grace,* was a peach orchard on the eastern shore of Maryland. Windy Hill was a real place, the home of my aunt and uncle, a place I spent many glorious summers. The same goes for the setting of my second novel, *The Cabin.* This one is set in the mountains of Virginia, another of my childhood haunts.

Stories are found in history. Some of the greatest books written are historical novels. Think of Phillipa Gregory's novel, *The Other Boleyn Girl,* or John Jake's North and South trilogy.

Recently, I edited a novel where one of the characters was talking about the Latin American holiday, Day of the Dead. The character was saying Day of the Dead was a time of terror, when people raped and pillaged and slaughtered people who ventured out of their house. This is, of course, factually inaccurate. Day of the Dead is a time to honor the dead, not add to their numbers. It is never okay to change facts in this way, especially when the "facts" aren't a major plot feature.

So when is it okay to change historical fact? When the plot of your novel asks the question, "What if things were different?" it is okay to rewrite history. For example, if your book asked the question, "What if Jesus had been a woman?" it's okay to change historical fact and make Jesus female. Or, if your premise is, "What if the South had won the Civil War?" it's okay to write a book to reflect this. But changing facts about history or cultural traditions and claiming it's okay because your book is fiction is not only wrong, it's going to make for disgruntled readers.

Stories are in the news. I once read a headline about a man who boxed himself into a shipping crate and had himself shipped via air express from New York to Texas. There's a story in there somewhere. Why did he ship himself in a box? Why didn't he take the train, or the bus? Was he running from something? Or running *to* something? These are the kinds of questions story writers ask themselves when they scan the headlines.

In short, stories are everywhere. Use your ears, your eyes. Most important, use your imagination.

If you don't already, start carrying a small notebook and pen with you wherever you go. When you see something interesting, jot it down! When you hear a snippet of conversation, or see a person who is behaving in a unique way, take notes. Nothing you notice that interests you is too mundane to note down. These little snippets of daily life are the tendons and capillaries and muscle tissue that will help you flesh out your story. You may even find the backbone of your tale in such an incident.

Don't rely on your memory to keep these images and words fresh in your mind. I can tell you from painful experience, it won't work. If you don't write them down right away, at least call yourself and leave a message on your voicemail detailing the interesting thing you saw or overhead. Your cell phone can become as useful a tool as your computer if you use it in this manner.

In the Beginning…

To some extent, how you begin your story depends on whether you are writing a literary, commercial, or genre novel, and whether you are writing for adults or for the young adult (YA, meaning teen and pre-teen) market. The literary novel has time to build momentum; commercial, genre, and young adult fiction by their very nature must drop the reader into a situation where the momentum is already in place. History is unfolded in the literary novel; in the others, the reader is dropped into a situation that already has a history. Literary novels may tell the entire history; commercial, genre, and young adult novels offer just a glimpse of history.

There are several interesting ways to start your story. You can begin in the middle, then backtrack and fill in details. This is often called a "frame story." You can begin with a Big Promise to fulfill (or not fulfill, as the case may be.) You can begin with action, with dialogue, with character description, or in the case of literary novels, with setting description.

But no matter how you choose to start your story, keep in mind **the best beginning poses a question, or questions, to the reader.** Questions posed should make the reader curious about your characters' motivation, or draw them into the story's central *conflict*. Every story *must* have conflict, something your characters are striving to achieve or overcome. Without conflict, your don't have a story; you have a character sketch. We'll talk more about this in our session on character development.

What do we mean by "opening" of your story? By opening, we're talking about the first few paragraphs or, at the most, the first scene. Why such a short section of your manuscript? Because, *you have only three pages to attract the attention of readers, editors, and publishers.* If you don't hook your reader from the get-go, they will not read on. Think about your own experience with selecting books to purchase at the bookstore. You open a book and glance over the first page or so to see if it grabs your interest, right? Publishers and editors do exactly the same thing. And trust me, opening with page after page of "setting up the story," as students often explain to me they are doing, will not hook a reader. (Take heart—you have three whole pages. Short story writers have only three *paragraphs* to do this.)

Let's look at these different methods of opening your story in a bit more depth:

Begin in the Middle:

Take this famous opening, an example of beginning in the middle, from Harper Lee's *To Kill a Mockingbird*:

> When he was nearly thirteen, my brother Jem got his arm badly broken at the elbow. When it healed, and Jem's fears of never being able to play football were assuaged, he was seldom self-conscious about his injury. His left arm was somewhat shorter than his right; when he stood or walked, the back of his hand was at right angles to his body, his thumb parallel to his thigh. He couldn't have cared less, so long as he could pass and punt.
>
> When enough years had gone by to enable us to look back on them, we discussed the events leading to his accident. I maintain that the Ewells started it all, but Jem, who was four years my senior, said it started long before that. He

said it began the summer Dill came to us, when Dill first gave us the idea of making Boo Radley come out.[1]

This excerpt obviously is an example of starting in the middle. The narrator—a young girl we later learn is named Scout—is reflecting back on the time several years early where the events unfolded in the story take place. Remember, the best story openings create questions in the mind of the reader. Has Harper Lee done this? Let's look at some of the questions the opening poses. How did Jem break his arm? Why is this important to the story? Who is Dill, and why did he come to visit one summer? Who is Boo Radley, and why would they want to make him come out? Come out from where? The most important question the opening poses in my mind is, who is narrating the story?

That's six questions posed by this opening, six reasons for the reader to continue on, searching for the answers.

Does this sentence drop the reader into a situation that already has a history? Clearly, yes. Something happened; the narrator speaks of "the events leading to his accident." And during the course of the story, what happens becomes clear.

Begin with Action:

Commercial, genre, and YA fiction must drop your reader into a situation where the momentum is already built. Plopping your reader into a scene already in motion is an excellent way to do this.

Let's look at the opening of Sarah Natalia Lee's YA novel, *Saving Amy*:

On the eastern outskirts of the expansive city, beyond the lights aglow like a hundred tiny stars in the vortex of blackness, nesting innocently in the comforts of the small, secure neighborhood, a tiny house slept in the middle of a small yard, its white sides glowing in the moonlight. A dog barked from across the street, and a slender figure darted from shadow to shadow, quick as a cat, across the dark lawn and to the sliding glass back door, where it came to a halt and looked in the window.

The young woman was standing in the kitchen, visible in the moonlight seeping through the windows, her legs bare and strong, her curvy torso covered by a lacy satin slip reaching just past her bottom. Her long blonde hair shone as she tipped her head back and let the water pour from the crystal glass into her mouth; her arm lifted to reveal the moderately sized ridge that was her breast line. Desire oozed through the creature's mouth; this one was so perfect, so young, so sexy; he knew he must have her. He waited impatiently until she put her glass on the counter and turned toward the door.

Her crystal blue eyes locked onto his and widened; her beautiful red lips opened in surprise and she slowly lifted her hand to her throat. He smiled satisfactorily; he had her.[2]

Does this opening pose questions to the reader? Yes. Who is this "creature" peeping through the sliding glass door? And just what does the author mean by "creature"? Who is the woman? What does it mean at the end, when it says "he had her"? Once again, the reader must continue on to find the answers.

Is the scene already in motion? Again, the answer is yes. The "creature" came from somewhere. Where was he before? What was he doing? And what was the woman doing before she looked up and saw him at the window? Not only does this scene begin in motion, that motion creates an entire new set of questions for the reader.

Begin with Dialogue:

Remember my saying by its very nature the genre and YA fiction must drop the reader into a situation where the momentum is already built? Starting with dialogue is an excellent way to accomplish this. Here is the opening of Alice Munro's *Open Secrets*:

> "And they almost didn't even go," Frances said. "Because of the downpour Saturday morning. They were waiting half an hour in the United Church basement and she says, Oh, it'll stop—my hikes are never rained out! And now I bet she wishes it had've been. Then it would've been a whole other story."[3]

Opening with dialogue drops us into a situation that already has a history, already has momentum, by dropping us into the middle of a conversation already taking place. It's like joining in a conversation that is already taking place at a cocktail party—you have to listen in for a few minutes to sort out what the discussion is about. This is exactly why opening with dialogue can work so well—the reader must read on to figure out what the conversation is about.

Notice that Munro artfully combined two opening styles into one, as this is not only an example of beginning with dialogue, but also of beginning in the middle.

What questions are posed the reader in Munro's opening? By now, you should be able to come up with at least a couple questions that need answers. See if you can figure them out for yourself this time.

Begin with Character Description:

With rare exception, fiction is character driven, meaning the action (or plot) is generated by what ever conflict the central character is experiencing. A good novel gets to the core of that conflict, giving the reader a glimpse of the central character's soul. Because of this, character description is often used to begin a story. Look at the opening of Ursula Hegi's novel, *Stones from the River:*

> As a child Trudi Montag thought everyone knew what went on inside others. That was before she understood the power of being different. The agony of being different. And

the sin of ranting against an ineffective God. But before that—for years and years before that—she prayed to grow.

Every night she would fall asleep with the prayer that, while she slept, her body would stretch itself, grow to the size of that of other girls her age in Burgdorf—not taller ones like Eva Rosen, who would become her best friend in school for a brief time—but into a body with normal-length arms and legs and with a small, well-shaped head. To help God along, Trudi would hang from door frames by her fingers until they were numb, convinced she could feel her bones lengthening; many nights she'd tie her mother's silk scarves around her head—one encircling her forehead, the other knotted beneath her chin—to keep her head from expanding.[4]

Notice this description doesn't tell us everything about Trudi's looks. We don't know her hair or eye color. We don't know how old she is, although clearly she is not a child. What we do know is she is unusually short, has arms and legs that are not normal length, and an unusually large head. Trudi is, in fact, *zwerg*, or dwarf, a term that isn't used until the reader is well into the book.

But what we know about Trudi from this opening goes far beyond recognizing her physical differences. We know what her state of mind was as a child, too—her differences were "agony" and she desperately wanted to change her appearance.

What questions does this opening pose?

Begin with Setting Description:

Novels that open with setting description are almost always literary in nature. This is because in the literary novel, setting takes on a major thematic role, like the ocean in *Moby Dick* or the jungle in *Mosquito Coast*. Remember, with commercial, genre, and young adult fiction, you want to drop your reader into a story that already has a history. You can't do this if you begin with setting description. With a literary novel, you have time for that history to unfold, and setting description is often used to open this kind of novel.

Let's look at the opening to Willa Cather's *O Pioneers!*:

One January day, thirty years ago, the little town of Hanover, anchored on a windy Nebraska tableland, was trying not to be blown away. A mist of fine snowflakes was curling and eddying about the cluster of low drab buildings huddled on the gray prairie, under a gray sky. The dwelling-houses were set about haphazard on the tough prairie sod; some of them looked as if they had been moved in overnight, and others as if they were straying off by themselves, headed straight for the open plain. None of them had any appearance of permanence, and the howling wind blew under them as well as over them. The main street was a deeply rutted road, now frozen hard, which ran from the squat red railway station and the grain "elevator" at the north end of the town to the lumber yard and the horse pond at the south end. On either side of this road straggled two uneven rows of wooden buildings; the general merchandise stores, the two banks, the drug store, the feed store, the saloon, the post-office. The board sidewalks were gray with trampled snow, but at two o'clock in the afternoon the shopkeepers, having come back from dinner, were keeping well behind their frosty windows. The children were all in school, and there was nobody abroad in the streets but a few rough-looking countrymen in coarse overcoats, with their long caps pulled down to their noses.[5]

What makes Cather's opening work is that it paints a color, three-dimensional picture of setting. True, the color is predominantly the gray of the sky and trampled snow, the unremarkable, non-descript prairie sod dwelling-houses, the white of snow swirling about. The only real flash of color is the red railway station. But the bleak illustration of setting is thematic of the story, representing the hard, dreary life and suffering experienced by settlers on the Nebraska frontier. Even the red train station is also thematic, representing Alexandra Bergson, the protagonist of the story. Alexandra is an unmarried pioneer woman, a lone female in a world dominated by men.

Once again, opening with setting is appropriate only for literary novels where setting is thematic. It isn't appropriate for opening commercial, genre, or young adult fiction.

No matter what method you choose for beginning your story, keep in mind your opening scene (in a short story) or chapter (in a novel) should do the following:

- Introduce the main character and give clear signals about his or her personality, appearance, flaws, and strengths. Force your reader to care about this character.

- Introduce, or at least allude to, the good guy's (called the *protagonist*) adversary (the "bad guy", or *antagonist*). Characterize him as well.

- Present or strongly suggest the conflicts of the story. In short story, there usually is only one conflict. A novel usually will have a main conflict and subconflicts, or *subplots*—the most important should come into play early in the story.

We will learn more about these things in the coming chapters. But keep them in mind as you do the exercises at the end of this chapter.

To Outline, or Not to Outline

Remember writing term papers in high school? You came up with a theme, then made a detailed outline of everything you wanted to cover in your paper. Only then did you dare put pen to paper (okay, I confess...I went to high school before the advent of the personal computer! I know how to use a slide rule, too, but that's another story) and write your report.

That worked fine for fact-filled term papers. For many fiction writers, though, outlines don't work. This is because a story is often discovered as it is written. You can't write an outline if you don't know what your characters are going to do.

Stories are character driven. Without characters, there is no story. But many beginning authors thing they have total control of their characters' actions and attributes. The truth is, *characters often take on a life of their own, and their lives take off in a different direction from the direction their creators intended.* When your characters try to lead you in surprising and unintended directions, let them! Usually, the characters know what they are doing.

When I was writing my first novel, *Redeeming Grace*, I started out with the intention of writing a love story. I had inherited a box of my deceased aunt and uncle's love letters written to each other when they were courting during the 1920's. This was going to be the backbone of my story.

But Grace and Otto, my two main characters, didn't want the book to be a love story, at least, not entirely. The final draft ended up being the story of a woman's desperate attempt to save her younger sister from their abusive father while examining and challenging the beliefs of her patriarchal religious upbringing. Is there a love story in there? Yes. But had I followed my plan to make the book a love story, and not followed Grace's lead when she took a different path, I doubt I would have had a saleable manuscript.

For this reason, I do not encourage my students to outline their stories before writing them. Old habits die hard. If you have an outline and are determined to stick with it, you may end up shutting out the voice of your characters when they try to lead you down the story's true path—their path.

That said, I realize there are some writers who totally disagree with this approach. Many fine writers outline their stories before committing them to paper. Some never waver from what they have outlined; others are flexible, and veer off course if the characters compel them to do so. If you feel you absolutely cannot write without an outline, by all means, go ahead and outline your story. Only time and experience will tell you whether this is a wasted exercise or not.

Exercises

1. Browse through your library and find three stories you like. What technique does the author use to

start his or her story? What questions are posed by the story openings? See if you can find examples of each opening technique discussed in this chapter.

2. Pick a favorite story and identify the technique the author used in the opening. This should be a book you are already familiar with. Now, rewrite the opening using the other techniques. For example, if the author started off by using action, try rewriting the scene beginning with dialogue. In your opinion, which style of opening works best for the story? Did the author get it right, or do you think a different opening style would have worked better?

3. If you have a story idea in mind—and I am assuming since you've purchased this book you do—write the opening few paragraphs of your story. Try different opening techniques. Does one jump out at you as being superior to the others?

CHAPTER 2

CHARACTERIZATION

Characterization is the cornerstone of a work of fiction. Without characters, you have no story. The action in your story is generated by whatever predicament the central character is in. And your characters *must* be in some sort of predicament. They must have **conflict**.

Conflict stems from one thing: desire. Your characters must want something, and want it badly. It can be something big, like to traverse the Appalachian Trail in a wheelchair, or to be the first tourist to the moon. Or, it can be something small, like rescuing an orphaned baby chipmunk and nursing it back to health. The important thing is not how big or small the desire is, but how badly your character wants it.

Characters must be ***multi-dimensional***. Flat, one-dimensional characters make for a boring read. You want your characters to feel real to your readers. Real people are multi-dimensional. They have their good points and their flaws, because no one is perfect. Your characters need these imperfections, too.

For example, your protagonist may be a kindly grandmotherly type who makes teddy bears for sick children at the community hospital. But get inside her home and you may find she's not thrown anything away for two decades, and that she lives in filth because none of her sixty-eight cats have been neutered.

Of course, this is a rather dramatic example. Character flaws can be less obvious—your character may chew her knuckles when she's nervous, for example, or have a short fuse in the temper department.

Just as your protagonist must have flaws, your antagonist must have redeeming qualities in order to be real. Take Hannibal Lechter from *Silence of the Lambs.* Pure evil, right?

Wrong. Like it or not, Lechter had some redeeming characteristics. He was intelligent, articulate, loved books and art, and had a father-like affection for Clarice Starling.

Characters must be a mixture of both **external** and **internal character traits**. External are probably the easiest to define, because these are things you can see. Hair color, physical build, gender, and other physical traits are examples of external traits you can see.

But external traits also include characteristics that may not be as obvious, like speech patterns (for example, a nasal voice, or an unusually lyrical voice) and mannerisms or habits. For example, if you were taking one of my community college workshops instead of reading this book, you'd find I pace back and forth while I lecture, and wave my hands around a lot. If I were a fictional character, these would be examples of external traits.

Internal traits are your character's personality traits, and his or her motivation vis-à-vis his or her conflict. Your character may be an eternal optimist, a miserly Scrooge, or frightened of his own shadow.

The best characters are those that display a balance of external and internal character traits. To distinguish your characters and make them memorable, character traits must also:

- *Be vivid*. Having messy long hair is not a vivid characteristic, because it doesn't create much of a visual image. Having 'what looked like a haystack where her hair should have been ' however, instantly creates an image in the reader's mind.

- *Be character-specific*. If a character has a nose like a gourd, he should be the only character with this unfortunate characteristic. Keep this in mind where you are naming your characters. Having your protagonist named Mary Ann Jones and your antagonist Marian Johnson is probably not a good idea, as the names are too similar and may create confusion in your readers' minds.

Whatever combination of traits you give your characters, before you start writing about them, you have to get to know them as well as you know yourself. You have to know not only what they look like, but where they work, where they grew up, what kind of car they drive. Do they have siblings? Pets? What is their favorite color? Food likes and dislikes? Do they have any medical problems? These are just a few of the things you might want to know about your characters before you start writing your story.

The best way to get to know your characters is to create a *characterization chart*. Think of this as sort of a resume for your characters. Here is an example of what your characterization chart might look like:

CHARACTERIZATION CHART

Name: _____

Age: _____

Height: _____

Weight: _____

Eye Color: _____

Hair Color: _____

Distinguishing Features:

_____

_____

_____

_____

Family Background:

_____

_____

_____

_____

Education:

_____

_____

_____

FRONT-WORD, BACK-WORD, INSIGHT-OUT

Religion: _____

Occupation: _____

Marital Status: _____

Children: _____

Favorite Color: _____

Favorite Food: _____

Habits (Good ones, bad ones, annoying ones):

_____

_____

_____

_____

Opinions:

_____

_____

_____

_____

Fears and Phobias:

_____

_____

_____

_____

Hobbies and Interests:

_____

_____

_____

_____

Health Issues:

_____

_____

_____

_____

Best Friend(s): _____

Car Make/Model: _____

Major Conflict that Must be Overcome:

_____

_____

_____

_____

_____

_____

_____

_____

_____

Create one for each of your major characters, and use it to get to know them. Tailor this to meet your characterization needs, or create one of your own.

Weaving Character Description Into Your Story

Once you've filled out your characterization chart, you're ready to share the wealth of information you've learned about your character with your readers. There's an art to doing this, however. One of the biggest errors writers can make is unloading too much about their characters all at once.

For example:

> Cheri was a thirty-three year old secretary who hated both her job and her roommate, whom she was certain was sleeping with her boyfriend.

In this sentence we learn our character's name, her age, her job, and her predicament (we'll assume since it says she hated her job and her roommate, she has the desire to fix these things). But how is the characterization? Boring! We learn nothing about Cheri's personality from this description, only raw facts. This is because it breaks the writer's mantra, that mantra being: **Show, don't tell.**

Let's rewrite the sentence, invoking this mantra:

After a nerve-wracking day of answering phones for Mr. Jones, typing and retyping quarterly financial statements, and standing at the Xerox machine nearly two hours copying, collating, and stapling twenty sets of deposition documents, Cheri dragged herself into the bar two doors down from her apartment building. She ordered a Red Stripe, which sat untouched while she chain smoked Camels and absentmindedly played with the stale peanuts that were set before her, compliments of the house. "Father Figure" was playing on the jukebox. She'd loved that song when she was in college, but once she found out George Michael was gay the song kind of lost its appeal.

She'd told both her roommate and her boyfriend she was going to visit her father this week-end, and she wondered just how long she'd have to wait before going home in order to catch Emily and the two-timing son-of-a-bitch in the sack together.

In this version, we get the same facts as the first version. We get her age—not exactly, but a rough estimate, because we know "Father Figure" was a popular song when she was in college. We get the idea she hates her job—after all, her day was so 'nerve-wracking' she 'dragged' herself to the bar. And we get a very clear picture of how she feels about her roommate.

But what else do we learn? For one thing, Cheri is one tough woman. She chain smokes Camels, and she's drinking beer, not wine or a martini. We get the idea she may not be the most tolerant person when it comes to gays. And we learn she's devious enough to stage an elaborate set-up for her roommate and boyfriend rather than simply confronting them about her fears.

Show, don't tell. It works for physical description, too. For example:

> Prince Charming was tall, dark, and handsome.

What does this tell us about Prince Charming? He's tall, as compared to what? Next to Frodo Baggins, Danny DeVito is tall. He's dark—does that mean suntanned? Or are they referring to his mood? And what does handsome mean? Princess Fiona thought Shrek was handsome, after all.

Let's try to come up with something better:

> The princess could see Prince Charming peering through the transom. His eyes, green as the shamrocks that grew in her garden, met her gaze, and it took the princess a moment to realize the light shining through the glass was not

a new star, but the most dazzling smile to ever grace the face of man, a smile made all the brighter when he ducked through the door and she could see it's contrast to his skin, which was the exact color of the coffee in her cup she held in her hand.

Okay, that's schmaltzy writing. Fairy tales aren't my forte. But you get the idea. We know the prince is tall because he is peering through a transom, which makes him at least taller than the door. We know he is handsome because of the princess's reaction to his smile, and that his skin is the color of coffee.

Here's an example from a real story. Look how Chester B. Himes opens his story, *Crazy in the Stir.*

The stained, squashed cigaret hanging from Red's tight lips glowed, a tiny spark in the yellow glare that spilled from the enameled reflector at the ceiling. Smoke dribbled from his mouth and nostrils, eddied upward around the cardboard sign that hung from the light by a string— "SPITTING ON THE FLOOR AND WALL FORBIDDEN."

Red put his hands palms downward on the gray blanket that was stretched out on the table and stood up, straddling the low, wooden bench. He spit the cigaret from his lips. It broke up, scattered tobacco flakes over the pasteboard poker chips piled in the center of the blanket.

The other six men in the game looked at him, looked away. He swung away from the game, moved down the aisle. The hard heels of his prison brogues made clumping sounds on the concrete floor. His tall, slim frame jerked stiffly as he walked. His hair was wild flame above his set, white face. His greenish-gray eyes were hot slits. Men walking up and down the aisle for exercise looked at his face, got out of the way.[6]

What do we learn from this description? We learn Red is tall, slim, red-haired, green-eyed, and incarcerated. We also learn the other inmates fear him.

But we can learn so much more than the obvious here. The squashed cigaret, the cardboard sign, the gray blanket and pasteboard poker chips create an undercurrent of cold despair. You suspect this is a prison before the fact is confirmed in the third paragraph.

When giving physical description, remember that you don't need to give every detail about a character's appearance. You need only give enough to leave a vivid impression in the reader's mind. Look how Flannery O'Connor does it, in her story A Good Man is Hard to Find:

> ...She wheeled around then and faced the children's mother, a young woman in slacks, whose face was as broad and innocent as a cabbage and was tied around with a green head-kerchief that had two points on the top like rabbit's ears. She was sitting on the sofa, feeding the baby his apricots out of a jar.[7]

O'Connor tells us nothing of the woman's hair color or height. We know she has on slacks, but we don't know what kind of blouse she's wearing, or if she has on shoes or is barefoot. We don't even know her name. She is referred to only as 'the children's mother'. Nevertheless, we have a vivid image of this cabbage-faced, rabbit-eared woman feeding her baby apricots.

In all the above examples, characterization is accomplished through *narration*. Narration is the author giving information to the reader, either directly, from the author's position outside the story, or through the eyes of a character/narrator.

But characterization can also be effectively conveyed through the use of *dialogue*. Dialogue, of course, is what your characters say out loud.

What do we learn about the father/daughter characters, Rosenfeld and Sophie, from this excerpt of Bernard Malamud's *Benefit Performance:*

He lit the flame under the vegetables and began to stir the mashed potatoes. They were lumpy. The remnants of his appetite disappeared. Sophie saw the look on his face and said, "Put some butter in the potatoes." For a moment Rosenfeld did not move, but when Sophie repeated her suggestion, he opened the ice box.

"What butter?" he said, looking among the bottles and the fruit. "Here is no butter."

Sophie reached for her housecoat, drew it on over her head and pulled up the zipper. Then she stepped into her slippers.

"I'll put some milk in," she said.

Without wanting to, he was beginning to grow angry.

"Who wants you to? Stay in bed. I'll take care myself of the—the supper," he ended sarcastically.

"Poppa," she said, "don't be stubborn. I've got to get up anyway."

"For me you don't have to get up."

"I said I have to get up anyway."

"What's the matter?"

"Someone is coming"

He turned towards her. "Who's coming?"

..."Ephraim."

"The plum-ber?" He was sarcastic.

"Please pa, don't fight."

"*I* should fight with a plum-ber?"

"You always insult him."

..."He insults *you* to come here. What does a plum-ber, who didn't even finish high school, want with you? You don't need a plum-ber."

"I don't care what I need, poppa, I'm twenty-eight years old," she said.

"But a plum-ber!"

"He's a good boy. I've known him for twelve years, since we were in high school. He's honest and he makes a nice steady living."

"All right," Rosenfeld said angrily. "So *I* don't make a steady living. So go on, spill some more salt on my bleeding wounds."

"Poppa, don't act, please. I only said *he* made a steady living. I didn't say anything about you."

"Who's acting?" he shouted, banging the ice box door shut and turning quickly. "Even if I didn't support you and your mother steady, at least I showed you the world...You heard the best conversation about life, about books and music and all kinds art. You toured with me everywhere. You were in South America. You were in England. You got a father whose Shylock in Yiddish even the American critics came to see and raved about it. *This* is living. *This* is life. Not with a plumber..."

"Poppa, that's not fair," she said quietly, "you make him afraid to talk to you."

The answer seem to satisfy him. "Don't be so much in the hurry," he said more calmly. "You can get better."

"Please, drop the subject."[8]

What do we learn about Rosenfeld through this dialogue? We learn he was, at one time, a fine actor. We learn he is now likely down on as luck, because he is living with his daughter and eating lumpy mashed potatoes for dinner. We learn he is scornful of his daughter's suitor, and thinks her seeing a plumber is beneath her.

And what of Sophie? Sophie is twenty-eight, and in 1943, when this story was written, being twenty-eight and single was not an enviable position for a woman to find herself in. She's living with her cantankerous father, caring for him, ducking his insults, and hoping with what comes across as quiet desperation he won't ruin her chances with her plumber boyfriend. Does she agree with her father's assessment the plumber isn't good enough for her? Perhaps—after all, the best she says in his defense is that he makes a steady living.

The advantage of using this technique for characterization (as opposed to saying something like <Rosenfeld was a domineering father, down on his luck, who was bound and determined to ensure his old-maid daughter was as miserable as he was>) is that is allows readers to come to this conclusion on their own. Readers are intelligent people. They don't like to be told what to think of characters. They want to determine for themselves what kind of people characters are, just as they do with real people in real life.

Show, don't tell. Three simple words that make or break a story.

Descriptive Language in Characterization

Some words of caution when writing character descriptions: Avoid overusing adjectives. One or two should suffice. For example, don't write sentences like:

Betsy ran the comb through her damp, tangled, shoulder-length, finely textured, straight, light ash blonde hair.

That's a bit exaggerated, of course, but you get the idea. Lengthy descriptions of character traits get boring, and you'll lose your readers.

Similarly, avoid clichés in your descriptions. Chiseled jaws, cornflower blue eyes, pouty red lips, and plumbers rear-ends sticking out when they bend over have all been done to death. (The expression "done to death" has been done to death, thus, is also cliché. Come up with fresh ways of describing your characters. How do you know if it's cliché or not? Did you write it yourself, or have you heard it said before? If it isn't a phrase of your own design, it's cliché.

Occasionally, I've had students attempt to get around having to describe their characters by comparing them to celebrities. For example:

Sarah was a dead ringer for Britney Spears.

Doing this is a mistake. For one thing, the author is assuming everyone knows what Britney Spears looks. That may be true today, but what about tomorrow? Celebrity comes and celebrity goes. Don't do your characters the disservice of comparing them to yesterday's news. It's lazy writing, and publishers and editors don't like it, figuring if you can't even describe your characters in an original way, why should they think you can tell a story in an original way?

Exercises

1.   Think of a favorite cartoon character—Bugs Bunny, Mickey Mouse, Kermit the Frog. Create a characterization chart for that cartoon character. You may use the one included in the earlier part of this chapter, or you may create your own. The purpose of this exercise is to familiarize you with the process of creating characterization charts using a character you already know well.

2.   Pretend you best friend (or your brother, or your aunt) is a character in a novel. Create a characterization chart for them.

CHAPTER THREE

SETTING

Many novice writers think the words 'scene' and 'setting' are interchangeable. They are not.

A *scene* is the action that takes place within a certain time, place, and from one character's viewpoint. A scene can be two sentences long, or several pages long. An entire chapter may have several scenes, or only one.

Any time you have a change in location, a jump in time, or switch to another character's viewpoint, you begin a new scene. New scenes are indicated by putting an extra return in your manuscript to create white space, like this:

Some writers put stars or some sort of little flourish between scenes, just to ensure readers understand there is a scene break, like this:

* * *

If you choose to do this (and I recommend this method), only three stars are necessary. You don't need a whole line of them.

Setting, on the other hand, is the location where the events of a scene take place. Setting could be a bedroom, a bar, or outer space.

Selecting the right setting for your story is crucial to the story's success. Would the novel *Gone With the Wind* have been successful if it had been set in London during World War II? *Fried Green Tomatoes at the Whistlestop Café* just wouldn't have been the same had Fannie Flagg instead written *Falafel Sandwiches at a Brooklyn Deli.*

Careful setting selection can make a story more suspenseful, comic, or intense, depending on what the writer is trying to achieve. For example, take the famous car chase scene from the movie *The French Connection* (movies are stories, too, after all, and the same principles often apply). Would the chase have had viewers perched on the edge of their seats had it taken place across the desert outside Las Vegas? No, because the suspense was created at least in part by the harrowing way the cars involved weaved in and out of traffic and between girders supporting the elevated train tracks. The risk of a major accident was always very real, a risk that wouldn't have been present had the chase taken place in the wide-open desert.

How much setting description do you need in a story? That depends on the story. You need enough description so your setting feels real to your readers, but you don't want to put in so much is slows down the action of your story.

In literary novels setting often takes on thematic significance, and lengthy setting descriptions are appropriate. Think of *Moby Dick*, for example, and Melville's lengthy descriptions of the sea. The sea is thematic, representing man's struggle with nature (with God), and therefore these descriptions are not only appropriate, but necessary to the story.

But commercial and genre fiction, as I have said before, are character driven. This means the setting will take a back seat to your characters and their actions. Lengthy descriptions are usually *not* necessary in genre fiction.

With setting description in genre and commercial, the saying 'less is more' is a good one to remember. Think of your story like it's a stage play, and your setting description your scenery. With most plays, setting is suggested by the careful selection of a few telling stage props.

If you have your character in a room, for example, don't feel compelled to detail every item of furniture, every painting on the wall, every dust bunny in the corner. A famous writer (sorry, I can't remember who it was) once said, "If there's a gun on the wall, it damn well better go off by the end of the story." That's good advice.

Let's look at an excerpt from my short story, *The Last Flight Home*:

> The river roars past me, slamming a fallen tree branch against a rock and splintering it into shreds before rushing over the granite shelf that is the top of the falls. Spray defies gravity, and water droplets hang mid air in a momentary state of suspended animation before plunging to the deep pool ninety feet below.
>
> I edge closer to the rim and look down. The pool looks different from up here, a bowl worried out of the granite over millions of years. Wondrous stuff, water. Soft enough to glide through without creating much more than a ripple, yet hard enough to shape the rock.[9]

This, of course, is a description of a river and waterfall. It is the only visual description of setting in the entire short story, which takes place in Great Smoky Mountains National Park. There is no attempt here to describe the trees, the sky, or the mountains. It's not necessary, because the river and the waterfall are my gun on the wall, so to speak.

Notice I say this is the only *visual* description of setting in the story. Visual descriptions, however beautiful and prosaic, paint a one-dimensional picture. Stories that rely on only visual descriptions lack texture But looks what happens when you add other senses to the mix. Let's pick up where we left off with *The Last Flight Home*:

> I close my eyes and take a slow, deep breath. These mountains have a scent all their own, a signature perfume. I've smelled it every time I've come here, but this time, I realize I can break down the individual essences perfuming the air: rotting rhododendron blossoms mixed with moss-covered granite and cold, crisp water. I've never before noticed that granite has a scent—like the air just before a storm, vaguely electrical—or that water smells cold.[10]

Here, rather than describing what she is seeing, my character narrator is describing what she is smelling. Yet this, too, is setting description, because it engages our sense of smell while at the same time, adding texture to the earlier visual imagery. We now know the rocks in the river are covered in moss and rhododendron is growing along the banks.

In Flannery O'Connor's story, *The Geranium*, we get a visual setting description in the opening paragraphs:

> Old Dudley folded into the chair he was gradually molding to his own shape and looked out the window fifteen feet away into another window framed by blackened red brick. He was waiting for the geranium. They put it out every morning about ten and they took it in at five-thirty. Mrs. Carson back home had a geranium in her window. There

were plenty of geraniums at home, better-looking geraniums...The geranium they would put in the window reminded him of the Grisby boy at home who had polio and had to be wheeled out every morning and left in the sun to blink.[11]

This is the only visual description of setting we get. Yet we get a much richer, more textured picture of Old Dudley's world when, several paragraphs into the story, O'Connor adds sound to her setting:

Somewhere down the hall a woman shrilled something unintelligible out to the street; a radio was bleating the worn music to a soap serial; and a garbage can crashed down a fire escape. The door to the next apartment slammed and a sharp footstep clipped down the hall.[12]

Whether you are writing about a totally fictitious place, your home town, or a place you visited or dream of visiting, you must do it convincingly. Remember, you want to convince your readers they are actually in the place you are writing about. It's called **willing suspension of disbelief**. Your readers want to believe what you are saying is true. But don't expect them to believe it just because you say it.

How do you convince your readers your setting is real? By doing your research before putting a word down on paper.

When the movie *Wayne's World* came out in 1992, I was living in Aurora, Illinois, the setting of the story. Aurora is suburban Chicago. It hits twenty below zero on a regular basis. Yet, in one scene of the movie, Wayne and his buddy Garth are driving down what is supposedly the main street of Aurora, and there are king palm trees lining the street! What's wrong with that image?

Similarly, what would be wrong with writing a short story where you had scarlet macaws flying over the jungles of Rwanda, or a murder mystery taking place on a dark, moonless July night in Stockholm, Sweden?

Willing suspension of disbelief will happen only if you get your facts right about your setting, and these "facts" are just plain wrong. Scarlet macaws are native to South America, not Africa. And it doesn't get very dark in the Land of the Midnight Sun, of which Stockholm is a part, in July. This is why you need to do your research before your start to write.

Does this mean everything about your story's setting must be factual? Of course not. If the action of your story takes place in a bar called O'Shannons on Chicago's Magnificent Mile, the fact that no such place exists isn't a problem. This is fiction, after all, and readers will understand there will be fictional places as well as fictional people. What you don't want to do, though, is put the Magnificent Mile in New York, or put the Seattle

Space Needle in Chicago; there can be no kangaroos on the Serengeti, and no white Christmas stories in Sydney, Australia.

Descriptive Language in Setting

Descriptive language is what distinguishes beautiful prose from the mundane. While this is true for every element of fiction writing, no where is it more true than with setting description.

Let's examine this sentence:

> There were trees on the other side of the river. In the distance you could see the city on the side of the mountain.

We get a picture here, of sorts. We know the narrator is standing on the bank of the river, and can see trees on the other side, as well as a city on the mountain side. But it's a rough sketch at best. We can't really picture the trees, because we don't know if they are evergreens, saplings, or old growth oaks. The sketch is also black and white. There's no color in it at all.

Let's see what happens to this black-and-white setting description in the hands of Flannery O'Connor in her story, *The River:*

Across the river there was a low red and gold grove of sassafras with hills of dark blue trees behind it and an occasional pine jutting over the skyline. Behind, in the distance, the city rose like a cluster of warts on the side of the mountain.[13]

Both descriptions are two sentences long, but how much clearer a picture do you get from O'Connor's description? We now see sassafras trees, their mitten-shaped leaves glowing red and gold in the autumn light. (We know it is autumn because otherwise the leaves would be green.) The red and gold is punctuated with splotches of dark green from the pine trees that dot her description. Do you think the narrator prefers the beauty of nature, or life in town? We can infer the former by the description of the city as a 'cluster of warts on the side of the mountain.'

Exercises

1.   Rewrite this classic but bland setting description:
      Over the meadow and through the woods to grandmother's house we go.

2.   Pretend your house or apartment is the setting for a murder mystery. Write two paragraphs describing the setting.

3.   Imagine your favorite place in nature. It could be a park, a garden, the ocean, a river—wherever you

have a had a magical moment in nature. Pretend this place is the setting for a story, and write a few paragraphs describing it. Remember to invoke all your senses!

4. This one is a bit more challenging: Write a paragraph of setting description where the senses of touch and smell are invoked.

Chapter Four

Point of View

You've decided to write a story. You've named your characters, chosen your setting, and figured out what the story's conflict will be. Now you have to decide who is going to tell the story. Usually, the narrator of the story is the person who has the most to win or lose, meaning your story's principal character. But sometimes it's better to have someone else tell the story because it allows for more suspense about the plot.

In novel writing, there is often more than one person telling the story. This is called using multiple viewpoint characters. Barbara Kingsolver's *The Poisonwood Bible* is an example of this. Each chapter is told from one of four character's viewpoint.

How do you decide whose perspective to use? Let's say you want to write a story inspired by the tragic crash of the Columbia space shuttle. In your story, the engineers analyze videotape of the heat shield tile falling off at lift-off and realize immediately the shuttle is going to crash when it re-enters Earth's orbit. The guys at mission control know the shuttle is going to crash, but choose not to tell the astronauts until just hours before re-entry. Do you tell the story from the viewpoint of one of the engineers? One of the guys at mission control? An astronaut? Doesn't sound like that big of deal, does it? Just pick one and get on with the story. But each viewpoint brings with it advantages and disadvantages, so selecting the proper one can completely change how the reader experiences the story.

Notice I say viewpoint, not point of view. In everyday life, the two terms are often used interchangeably. We say point of view when what we really mean is viewpoint.

In fiction, **viewpoint** means the character's perspective being presented. **Point of view (POV)** means how the story is written.

In general, there are four different types of POV: first person; second person; third person limited; and third person unlimited, which is also known as omniscient POV.

First Person POV:

In first person POV, the story is told through the eyes of the narrator, using the personal pronouns "I," "me," and "my." Events that unfold in a first person story are limited to what the narrator can observe, and to the narrator's emotional life and psychological state.

First person seems to be the favored POV choice among beginning writers and is a popular choice of writers at all skill levels. One reason for this is its almost confessional tone. It's like the narrator is your best friend, confiding some big secret to you and you alone, taking you into his or her confidence.

Look at the following excerpt from Isaac Bashevis Singer's *Gimpel the Fool:*

> I am Gimpel the fool. I don't think myself a fool. On the contrary. But that's what folks call me. They gave me the name while I was still in school. I had seven names in all: imbecile, donkey, flax-head, dope, glump, ninny, and fool. The last name stuck. What did my foolishness consist of? I was easy to take in. They said, "Gimpel, you know the rabbi's wife has been brought to childbed?" So I skipped school. Well, it turned out to be a lie. How was I supposed to know? She hadn't had a big belly. But I never looked at her belly. Was that really so foolish? The gang laughed and hee-hawed, stomped and danced and chanted a good-night prayer. And instead of the raisins they give when a woman's lying in, they stuffed my hand full of goat turds. I was no weakling. If I slapped someone he'd see all the way to Cracow. But I'm really not a slugger by nature. I think to myself: Let it pass. So they take advantage of me.[14]

Notice the narrator immediately shares a traumatic, embarrassing moment with the reader—the kind of moment most people would share only with a close friend. This creates empathy for the narrator, and a bond is created between reader and Gimpel. We also learn Gimpel believes he could defend himself against from the onslaught of teasing and practical jokes, but chooses not to because of his nature. Rationalization? Or could he really stand up for himself if he chose to?

First person narrators may be reliable or unreliable. **Reliable narrators** are those you know to be telling the truth about events. Their telling of the story is not swayed by emotions, prejudice, or any other sort of bias. A narrator is considered reliable if nothing in the story contradicts his or her interpretation of the story's events.

Unreliable narrators, however, cannot be relied upon to tell the truth. They tell their version of the truth, of course, but that version may be swayed by emotions, prejudice, or some other sort of bias.

Let's look at the opening of Kurt Vonnegut's *The Barnhouse Effect*:

> Let me begin by saying that I don't know any more about where Professor Arthur Barnhouse is hiding than anyone else does. Save for one short, enigmatic message, left in my mailbox on Christmas Eve, I have not heard from him since his disappearance a year and a half ago.[15]

This is, of course, a first person POV story, because the narrator uses the personal pronoun "I." Remember at the beginning of this chapter I said that usually, the narrator of the story is the person who has the most to win or lose, meaning your story's principal character, but that sometimes it's better to have someone else tell the story because it allows for more suspense about the plot? This is the case in Vonnegut's story. Professor Barnhouse is the principal character; the narrator is his sidekick. Is he a reliable narrator? Yes, because nothing in the story contradicts his assertion that he doesn't know where Barnhouse is hiding.

Compare this to an excerpt from my story, *Good-bye, Emily Dickinson*:

There's a big granite rock at the edge of the park engraved with the names of the forty-two men from town who have died defending our country—more proof that greatness is not appreciated until after a person is dead.

My husband's name is number forty-one on the list. Walter E. Jorgens, Private First Class. Walter died in Viet Nam when some drunken fool from his own platoon tossed a grenade at the privy. Walter died with his pants down, two days before the war ended and his unit returned home.

I held my head high like a grieving widow should. But I saw how people snickered and whispered behind my back about Walter's embarrassing demise. That nearly killed me, being laughed at like that. Before Walter died, I was a respected citizen in this town. In the years following his death,

I became a pariah. I had to quit my job—I taught freshman literature at the high school—because my students would look at me like I was speaking in tongues while standing naked in front of them. I knew what they were thinking. They were thinking what a fool I must have been, being married to a guy who got himself blown up in a privy.

I complained to the principal, and he sat in on a few of my classes. He said he didn't see what my problem was. That's when I realized he, too, took me for a fool. I quit on the spot.[16]

This, too, is a first person story. Emily is a homeless woman who suffers from paranoid delusions, and who believes she is the daughter of Emily Dickinson. Do the events of the story really take place as she tells it? Were people really whispering behind her back? We cannot know for sure, because she is an unreliable narrator due to her mental illness.

One of the biggest problems beginning writers have with first person POV is inadvertently putting in the thoughts of characters other than the viewpoint character (narrator). Remember, in first person POV you can write only what the viewpoint character can observe. Readers of *Good-bye, Emily Dickinson* will never know, for example, what the principal was really thinking when he sat in on Emily's classes. She could *assume* he thought she was a fool, but she cannot know that for a fact. Readers of *Gimpel the Fool* can't know what is going on in the heads of the people who torment Gimpel because it is told from his perspective, not the perspective of his tormentors. Gimpel can guess at the reasons, but because he cannot observe their thoughts, his guesses are just that—speculation.

Second Person POV:

If the narrator uses the personal pronoun "you," he is using second person POV. This is extremely rare in novels, and while it supposedly is a bit less rare in contemporary short story, a search through nearly a dozen short story collections on my own library shelves turned up not a single short story written in second person POV. This should tell you something: Second person POV is probably not a good choice for beginners.

Novelists sometimes interrupt stories written in first or third person POV with a scene written in second person when they wish to address another character in the novel, but who is not present in the scene. For example, Vladimir Nabakov's Humbert Humbert addresses his love-interest, stepdaughter Lolita, like this:

> I would forget all my masculine pride and literally crawl on my knees to your chair, my Lolita! You would give me one look..."Oh no, not again...puelease, leave me alone, will you," you would say, "for Christ's sake, leave me alone."[17]

Notice the tone of this passage, the ironic bitterness about it. This feeling of removal, this bitterness, is one of the defining characteristics of second person POV.

Second person POV can also take a the confiding tone usually associated with first person POV. This was especially true in 19th century literature, where authors often interrupted their stories to address their readers:

> Marley was dead as a doornail. Mind! I don't mean to say that I know, of my own knowledge, what there is particularly dead about a doornail. But the wisdom of our ancestors is in the simile; and my unhallowed hands shall not disturb. You will therefore permit me to repeat, emphatically, that Marley was dead as a doornail.[18]

That, of course, is an excerpt from the opening of *A Christmas Carol*; the 'you' Dickens is addressing is the reader.

Probably the most familiar recent example of a novel written in second person POV is Jay McInerney's novel, *Bright Lights, Big City*, which begins:

> You are not the kind of guy who would be at a place like this at this time of morning. But here you are, and you cannot say that the terrain is entirely unfamiliar, although the details are fuzzy. You are at a nightclub talking to a girl with a shaved head. The Club is either Heartbreak or The Lizard

Lounge. All might become more clear if you could just slip into the bathroom and do a little more Bolivian marching powder. Then again, it might not. A small voice inside you insists that this epidemic lack of clarity is a result of too much of that already.[19]

In *Bright Lights, Big City*, the 'you' refers to the protagonist, who, as shown in this opening paragraph, is a junkie. But since in second person POV the pronoun 'you' also sometimes refers to the reader, on a subconscious level readers may feel McInerney is referring to *them* as junkies. It makes us uncomfortable, and creates emotional distance from the characters.

This feeling of discomfort is just one reason second person POV is unpopular with both readers and writers. Another reason is that its rarity makes it less familiar, and this makes readers uncomfortable.

I repeat: second person POV is not a good choice for beginners.

Third Person POV:

If the narration uses the personal pronouns "he," "she," or "they," the story is written in third person POV. There are two basic classifications of third person POV: *limited* and *unlimited*, or *omniscient*. Third person limited can be further broken down into *outer limited* (sometimes called 'fly-on-the-wall' perspective), and *inner limited*.

Third person unlimited, or *omniscient, POV* is the godlike approach that allows the reader to move around from character to character, and even backward and forward in time and space. For example, we may be experiencing an argument from the perspective of the character instigating the fight, and the very next sentence be in the perspective of the character on the receiving end. Steve Martin chose to use this POV for his novella (short novel, or long short story), *Shopgirl*, and did so in a brilliant comedic fashion. In this scene, Mirabelle and her older date, Ray Porter, are on their second date:

"I think I should tell you a few things. I don't think I'm ready for a real relationship right now." He says this not to Mirabelle but to the air, as though he is just discovering a truth about himself and accidentally speaking it aloud.

Mirabelle answers, "You had a rough time with your divorce."

Understanding. For Ray Porter, that is good. She absolutely knows that this will never be long term. He goes on: "But I love seeing you and I want to keep seeing you."

"I do too," says Mirabelle. Mirabelle believes he has told her that he is bordering on falling in love with her, and Ray believes she understands that he isn't going to be anybody's boyfriend.

"I'm traveling too much right now," he says. In this sentence, he serves notice that he would like to come into town, sleep with her, and leave. Mirabelle believes that he is expressing frustration at having to leave town and that he is trying to cut down on traveling.

"So what I'm saying is that we should be allowed to keep our options open, if that's okay with you." At this point, Ray believes he has told her that in spite of what could be about to happen tonight, they are still going to see other people. Mirabelle believes that after he cuts down on his traveling, they will see if they should get married or just go steady.[20]

Third person inner limited POV differs in that it limits what the reader sees to the perspective of one character at a time. What that one character thinks, sees, hears, feels, all can be written in third person limited POV. What you *cannot* do is write what other characters see, hear, think, and feel. You are limited to only what your viewpoint character can experience, just as you are with first person POV. If in *Shopgirl* Martin had chosen to use third person limited, the above scene would lose its comic effect, because we'd know only what Mirabelle was thinking (if she was the viewpoint character), or what Ray Porter was thinking (if he was the viewpoint character). What makes the scene so funny is having both their thoughts out there at the same time, something that can be done only by using omniscient POV.

Here's an excerpt from Truman Capote's chilling tale, *Miriam*:

"Look," said Mrs. Miller, rising from the hassock, "look—if I make some nice sandwiches will you be a good child and run along home? It's past midnight, I'm sure."

"It's snowing," reproached Miriam. "And cold and dark."

Well, you shouldn't have come here to begin with," said Mrs. Miller, struggling to control her voice. "I can't help the weather. If you want anything to eat you'll have to promise to leave."

Miriam brushed a braid against her cheek. Her eyes were thoughtful, as if weighing the proposition. She turned toward the bird cage. "Very well," she said, "I promise."[21]

In *Miriam*, Mrs. Miller is the viewpoint character. As such, we can get a glimpse at her psychological state, as she struggles to control her voice. We do not, however, get any idea of what is going on inside Miriam. We can't, because we can only know what Mrs. Miller, as the viewpoint character, can observe about her. Notice the careful wording in this sentence: <Her eyes were thoughtful, as if weighing the proposition.> Mrs. Miller can see Miriam's eyes, can see what she interprets as a thoughtful look. What Mrs. Miller cannot know is why Miriam has a thoughtful look. She interprets it as Miriam weighing the proposition set before her. <Her eyes were thoughtful, *as if* weighing the proposition.> The words 'as if' convey this as Mrs. Miller's opinion, not an actual statement of fact about Miriam's thoughts.

In *third person outer limited*, or *fly-on-the-wall POV*, the author writes in a completely objective manner and presents only what can be observed externally. The author has to use descriptions of behavior and dialogue to convey the characters' personalities. Character thoughts, unspoken desires, and motivations are not written, because these things cannot be observed externally. Instead, the reader must interpret the events of the story in order to deduce the character's motivations and desires.

Ernest Hemingway was a master at writing in third person outer limited POV. Take a look at this excerpt, from *Big Two-Hearted River.*

> The train went on up the track out of sight, around one of the hills of birch timber. Nick sat down on the bundle of canvas and bedding the baggage man had pitched out of the door of the baggage car. There was no town, nothing but the rails and burned over country. The thirteen saloons that had lined the one street...had not left a trace. The foundations of the hotel stuck up above the ground. The stone was chipped and split by the fire. It was all that was left of the town.[22]

Notice there is no mention of what Nick thinks of this sight. We don't know if it startles him, surprises him, or saddens him. We know only that he got off the train and observed the town's ruin. Hemingway's description is totally objective.

Third person outer limited POV is challenging—even Hemingway slipped occasionally while attempting to write stories in third person outer limited. For this reason, it probably isn't the wisest choice for a novice writer.

POV Slips:

Once you choose your POV, convention dictates you stick with that POV for the duration of each scene or chapter of your story. With longer stories and novels, you can change viewpoint characters, and even switch from one POV to another (from first person to third person inner limited, for example). When can you do this? Only when you begin a new scene or, in the case of a novel, a new chapter.

The idea of telling a story from inside a particular character's head seems easy enough, but it's harder than you may think—even experienced writers slip on occasion. Writing in omniscient POV is one thing; planting your readers solidly in one character's viewpoint and then suddenly starting to write things the viewpoint character can't possibly know is called head-hopping, or a POV slip.

POV slips can be as obvious as telling us what a non-viewpoint character is thinking, or as subtle as saying <Sally ran happily into the room> when Sally isn't the viewpoint character. (You can't say Sally was happy if she isn't the viewpoint character, because your viewpoint character can't know Sally is happy simply by the way she runs. She may have been running from a swarm of killer bees.)

You may be thinking "Aha! I'll always write in third person omniscient POV, and then I won't have to worry about making POV slips." Nice try, but no. Omniscient POV is not appropriate for most stories. This is an appropriate POV choice only when it is imperative to know what is going on in the heads of your main characters.

So how do you know what POV to use? The best way to decide this is to try writing the same scene using the different kinds. Try writing in first person, then writing in third person limited. Which sounds better to you? Which makes more sense?

There was a time when writers were told, "Pick a POV and stick with it throughout your novel." That's old advice, and not always followed anymore. You may find you like to do scenes or chapters where your protagonist is done in first person, and scenes or chapters where the other characters are in third person limited. Or, try doing the antagonist in first person and the others in third. Play around and see what feels right for you.

Once you decide, it is important to stick with your choice throughout the duration of your novel. For instance, if you decide to do your protagonist in first person and everyone else in third, you should carry this through your entire book so you don't confuse your readers.

Ultimately, there is no right or wrong choice when it comes to POV. It's up to you, the writer, to decide what is right for your story.

Exercises

Read the following scene:

I dashed through the door to the train station; Samantha lagging eight steps behind me, taking her own sweet time, as usual. The woman is slower than the U.S. economy. It drives me absolutely nuts sometimes. I turn back, grab her by the arm, and drag her toward the coffee counter.

"We have only six minutes," I say, tapping my watch. "We're going to have to make a run for it, so don't order anything that you can't run with."

"Welcome to Espresso Express-O. Can I take your order?" The skinny teen behind the register must be going through some kind of voice change; his greeting sounds like a songbird that fell in a whiskey barrel.

"Coffee, half-caf, and a blueberry muffin." I turn to Sam. "Whattaya want?"

She stared at the menu, chewing her lower lip in that annoying manner of hers. "What's in an frozen Express-O supreme?"

"I dunno; it a premixed frozen coffee drink," the kid said, nodding toward the frozen beverage dispenser.

"Well, can you find out?"

I'll have to ask the manager," says the kid. "Hey Joe, what's in a supreme?"

I groan and tap my watch again. "If we miss the train, I'm gonna be late for court. We gotta move now, Sam. I mean it."

The manager strolls over to the counter and hands Carol a booklet, "Espresso Expresso-O Nutritional Information." She leafs through it, scanning each page like it's the most fascinating book she's ever read.

"Ooh, too many calories in a supreme," she says. "Can I have a corn muffin and an iced green tea latte instead? Made with skim milk."

The kid scratched his head. "The tea lattes are pre-mixed. I think they're made with two percent, not skim. We'll have to make one up special."

"Thank you, I'd appreciate it," Sam said.

I groan again. "Three minutes thirty-seven seconds. We're doomed."

1. Rewrite this scene with Samantha is the viewpoint character, once again using first person POV.

2. Rewrite the scene again, but this time, from the perspective of the teenager working behind the counter. Use third person inner limited POV.

CHAPTER FIVE

DIALOGUE

Dialogue is your characters speaking out loud. Most often, dialogue is distinguished by the use of **quotation marks** around the spoken words ("Pass the butter, please.") and the use of **tag lines.** ("Pass the butter, please," Jane said.)

Using dialogue in your story has several advantages. Remember from Chapter One I said most stories should drop the reader into a situation that already has a history; with momentum already building? Dialogue is one way to do this. Dialogue gives a story immediacy. It places readers at the site of a conversation where they can listen in as the conversation takes place.

dialogue in your short story has several advantages.

Dialogue also, you will recall from Chapter Two, is an effective tool in characterization. Remember the father/daughter characters, Rosenfeld and Sophie, from excerpt of Bernard Malamud's *Benefit Performance*?

The fiction writer's mantra is **show, don't tell**. Dialogue is an excellent way to invoke this mantra. In Flannery O'Connor's *A Good Man is Hard to Find*, a family on vacation, nervous already because a convicted murderer has escaped from prison and is headed in the same direction, has just had a car accident. They are standing around, wondering what to do, when they are approached by a group of men.

Let's imagine what O'Connor might have written about what happens next if she used narrative:

> As the family stood looking at their wrecked car, a group of men approached. One of the boys wondered why the men were carrying guns. As the father began to explain to the men the predicament they were in, the grandmother started shrieking that she recognized one of the men as the escaped convict called The Misfit. The Misfit said it would have been better if she hadn't recognized him.

All the information is there, but so what? The narrative is boring and bland. It expresses no emotion at all. Fortunately, Flannery O'Connor was a master storyteller who knew when to use dialogue. Let's see what she really wrote following the car accident:

> "We turned over twice!" said the grandmother.

"Oncet," he corrected. "We seen it happen. Try their car and see will it run, Hiram," he said quietly to the boy with the gray hat.

"What you got that gun for?" John Wesley asked. "Whatcha gonna do with that gun?"

"Lady," the man said to the children's mother, "would you mind calling them children to sit down by you? Children make me nervous. I want all you all to sit down right together there where you're at."

...Behind them the line of woods gaped like a dark open mouth. "Come here," said their mother.

"Look here now," Bailey began suddenly, "we're in a predicament! We're in..."

The grandmother shrieked. She scrambled to her feet and stood staring. "You're The Misfit!" she said. "I recognized you at once!"

"Yes'm," the man said, smiling slightly as if he were pleased in spite of himself to be known, "but it would have been better for all of you, lady, if you hadn't of reckernized me."[23]

Boring and bland? Hardly! Chilling? Absolutely. The piece is loaded with emotion, because O'Connor *shows* the emotions—The Misfit being nervous because of the children, Bailey (the father) anxiously trying to explain their predicament, the grandmother impulsively shrieking when she recognizes The Misfit.

Notice O'Connor also works a bit of setting description in this excerpt. The description of the woods that <gaped like a dark open mouth> is ominously foreshadowing of things to come.

What makes O'Connor's dialogue work is that it is compelling. One common mistake among beginning writers is they try to include dialogue that isn't compelling. It doesn't work, as illustrated here:

> Maxine was reading a book when the telephone interrupted her reverie.
>
> "Hello?" Maxine queried.
>
> "Hello, Maxine, this is your brother Tom. How are you?" Tom asked.
>
> "I am fine. How are you, Tom?" Maxine replied.
>
> "I am fine Maxine. How are the kids?" Tom countered.
>
> "The kids are fine. How's Beth?" Maxine inquired of Tom's wife.
>
> "Beth's fine. Say, Maxine, I wonder if you want to meet me at Shady Oaks Retirement Center, where Mom lives, at five o'clock on Friday. As you know, Maxine, Friday is Mom's birthday."
>
> "I'd be happy to meet you then, Tom," Maxine answered. "I'll see you then."
>
> "Good-bye, Maxine."
>
> "Good-bye, Tom."

Is this compelling dialogue? Hardly. The first six lines or so are the back-and-forth exchange of pleasantries that begin every conversation. You don't need to put them in your dialogue because readers know pleasantries are normally exchanged at the beginning of a phone conversation, or when two people meet.

Look at the information conveyed in the dialogue. The caller identifies himself as Maxine's brother Tom. The reader probably didn't know up until this time that Maxine had a brother Tom, but certainly Maxine knows it! And certainly Maxine doesn't need to be told their mother lives at Shady Oaks Retirement Center, or that she has a birthday on Friday. (That is, unless she is a very neglectful daughter!) In fact, the entire conversation seems to take place for the sole reason of conveying information about the characters to the reader that the characters themselves already know. This sort of "As you know" discourse is deadly to a story.

Another problem with this dialogue is the tag lines. Tag lines, or **attributions**, are the "he said", "she said" that accompany a line of dialogue. The rule for tag lines is, **the simpler, the better**. Never use a word other than "said" unless you have a compelling reason to do so. In the dialogue above, we have Tom and Maxine querying, asking, replying, countering, inquiring, and answering. Just reading all those tag lines is exhausting!

Another rule for tag lines: **use tag lines only when necessary to distinguish which character is speaking**. In the above phone conversation, there are only two people speaking, Maxine and Tom. We know the phone interrupted Maxine's reading, so a simple "Hello?" with no tag line would have been fine. After Tom identified himself, the reader would know who was on the other end of the phone, and virtually all ensuring tag lines become redundant. ***Use tag lines only when you need one to avoid reader confusion***.

Where do you put tag lines? In the above discourse, the end of the sentence is fine, because the sentences are short. But what if you had a section of dialogue that started like this:

> "I just don't know what to do about John. He's always hanging with the wrong crowd, like those weirdos from Baytowne, the ones that dress all in black and dye their hair fluorescent purple and drive around in that psychedelic painted hearse," Mary said.

The problem with this is, readers have to wait until the end of a very long speech to know who is speaking. If we know who is making the speech, we don't need a tag line at all. If we don't know, however, we need to know sooner. The rule with tag lines is, ***if you need to use a tag line, put it in as soon as is stylistically practical***. The above bit of dialogue would be must better if the tag line followed the first sentence:

"I just don't know what to do about John," Mary said. "He's always hanging with the wrong crowd, like those weirdos from Baytowne, the ones that dress all in black and dye their hair fluorescent purple and drive around in that psychedelic painted hearse."

Putting the tag line there allows the reader to concentrate on what is being said rather than wondering who is saying it.

Alas, even moving, simplifying and/or removing tag lines would not save the dialogue between Maxine and Tom, because it is not compelling. Their entire exchange could be summed up in one narrative line:

Maxine and Tom made arrangements to meet at Shady Oaks Retirement Center at five o'clock on Friday to celebrate their mother's birthday.

Remember, only write as dialogue things that are compelling. You don't like to talk to boring people, do you? Your readers don't want to read boring dialogue for the same reason.

Mixing Action With Dialogue

In real life, dialogue doesn't take place while people stand stiff as the guards at Buckingham Palace. People play with their hair, take a bite out of a sandwich, scratch an itch, or fiddle with the radio dial while carrying on a conversation. Your fictional characters should, too. Read the following example:

Charlie found his grandmother sitting at the kitchen table, playing solitaire. "You can't play a red six on a red seven, Granny," he said, setting the basket of crabs next to her on the floor. "Red goes on black. You play opposite colors."

"You play it your way; I'll play it mine." Florence placed the red seven onto a black eight before turning her face upward.

Charlie planted a dry kiss on her cheek, taking care not to scratch her with his chapped lips. "But you're cheating."

"Only myself, dear. What nice crabs; are they for me?" Red ten to black jack to black king to red ace.

"If you invite me to stay for supper. You missed the queen."

"Your point is?" She moved the last red king to red ace, and gave a chuckle of satisfaction. "There, I win! Get the crab kettle out of the pantry and put in on the stove for me, will you dear?"

This scene sounds realistic for two reasons: it isn't taking place in a vacuum, meaning the characters are moving around. Florence is playing cards, Charlie is setting down the crab basket, then kissing Florence. In addition, it sounds realistic because there are two conversations going on at once: one about the card game, and one about the crabs and Charlie staying for dinner.

How many tag lines did I use in the above bit of dialogue? Count them. There is only one. But there never is any question about who is talking, because I have substituted actions for tag lines to indicate who is talking. Replacing most of your tag lines with actions will not only tighten up your writing, it will give the reader a picture of what your characters are doing while they are talking.

Notice I use the word *realistic* to describe dialogue, not *real*. In real dialogue—the conversations that take place between real people—the spoken words are punctuated with stuttering, pauses, and interjections like *um*, *er*, and *ah*. If you put every stutter, every pause, every *um* in your fictional characters' dialogue that real people say in their own conversations, your characters will sound like illiterate, bumbling idiots. This is why we aim for *realistic*, not *real*, in dialogue.

Realistic dialogue also means using contractions. When we learn to write in grammar school, we're taught not to use contractions, at least not in formal papers. But people talk in contractions all the time. We don't say, "What is up, doc?" We say "What's up, doc?" I'll admit it— this is something I struggle with to this day. I always go back and read my dialogue aloud. This way I can hear if it sounds stiff and formal because of not using contractions, and I can go back and fix them.

When was the last time you heard someone say something like, "You know, Smoky, I read your book, and Smoky, I thought it was really good. I'd like to read your other books, Smoky." Sounds funny when you read it out loud, doesn't it? The fact is, when we are conversing with someone, we rarely call them by their name. Yet authors put names into dialogue like they put pepperoni on their pizza—liberally. This, too, I am guilty of, but, like finding missing contractions, these errors can easily be identified if you simply read your dialogue out loud.

Which brings us to the topic of dialect. Unless you are very familiar with the dialect your are attempting to elicit, it is better to suggest dialect than actually try to imitate it. Writing too heavy-handed dialect can lose readers, because they get frustrated trying to figure out what it is exactly the characters are trying to say. Let's say, for example, your short story is set in Atlanta and you are trying to convey a southern accent. Throw in the word *y'all* or the phrase *might could* at carefully chosen places suggest a way of speaking unique to southerners because they are expressions normally used only by southerners. Remember, readers are smart. Once they realize the character is a southerner, they'll hear the southern accent without you mangling the language.

Style Issues and Dialogue

During my tenure as a writing instructor, I've seen more variations on style issues with dialogue than any other aspect of fiction writing. This book assumes the reader has a working knowledge of punctuation and style. If you don't have a firm grasp on these issues, go out and purchase *The Chicago Manual of Style.* It is the writer's bible when it comes to punctuation, capitalization, and other issues that trip people up. No writer's library should be without this book.

There are a few errors writers make so consistently, however, that I will touch briefly on them here:

- ***Dialogue is indicated by putting quotation marks around the spoken words****. Quotation marks are used only for words spoken out loud. They are **not** placed around thoughts. Ever. Thoughts are indicated either by putting the thought in italics, or by adding a tag line such as 'he thought,' like this:

> Eeyore stared at the gray sky. It's going to be another gloomy day, he thought.
>
> OR
>
> Eeyore stared at the gray sky. *It's going to be another gloomy day.*

Recently, there has been a trend toward a third option for thoughts, using both the italics and the tag line.

> Eeyore stared at the gray sky. *It's going to be another gloomy day,* he thought.

I've seen all three styles used in novels I've read recently. Seems like every publisher has their own style they follow when it comes to thoughts. While writing your book, pick a style for thoughts and be consistent with its use. If you go for roman type with the "he thought" tag line, use that throughout. If you use italics with the tag line, use that throughout. Consistency is more important than which style you use.

- **You must use terminal punctuation at the end of a line of dialogue.** The terminal punctuation, whether it is a period, comma, question mark, or exclamation point goes *inside* the close-quotation mark:

> "Let's get some lunch," he said.
> Gerry said, "Let's get some lunch."
> "Let's get some lunch," Gerry said, "then go to the movies."

- *Only one piece of terminal punctuation per bit of dialogue*. I've seen writers put commas with question marks, commas with exclamation points, question marks with exclamation points, and multiple (!!!) exclamation points. The rule is, *only one*. And take it easy with using any exclamation points at all. If you feel compelled to use a lot of exclamation points, you need to take another look at your writing to see if you are using strong enough verbs to elicit the excitement you are trying to project with punctuation. Words, not punctuation, are how good writers show excitement.

Exercises

1. Write a scene where an angel and the devil meet and have a conversation on the beach in Hawaii, where both are vacationing. Remember to include characterization and setting description, but your primary focus should be the dialogue.

2. Find a favorite excerpt of dialogue from a book in your library. Identify who the viewpoint character is. Then, rewrite the dialogue from the other character's viewpoint.

CHAPTER 6

PLOT DEVELOPMENT

Remember building block cities as a child? Your skyscrapers may have been three or four blocks high. Stores and schools might have been two or three blocks high, and houses only one or two blocks high.

Each block by itself was just that—a block. Alone, it was a humble piece of wood. But put a bunch of them together, and you had a city.

In writing, scenes are the building blocks for our stories. All stories are a compilation of scenes. In a novel, you may have hundreds or thousands of scenes.

When putting your scenes together, keep in mind your story doesn't have to unfold in a linear fashion. While children's books always are linear, YA and adult novels usually contain *flashbacks.* A flashback is when a character is remembering something from the past that is pertinent to the story unfolding. This is an excellent way to introduce back story, rather than "setting the scene" at the beginning of your book—which, but now. you already know you shouldn't do.

Here is an example of a scene containing a flashback, from my short story, *Breathe*:

"You're so full of shit, Armondo," Daisy said, twisting sideways in her chair and tossing her legs casually over the arm rest. "You left out a key part of the story."

"Like what?"

"Like the fact you forgot to pick me up at the airport."

Okay, so maybe I didn't quite tell the whole truth. We were unlucky enough to live in a county that required marriage counseling before a couple could divorce, but that didn't mean I wanted to be there, coming off as a total jerk in front of some court-appointed shrink.

I didn't exactly forget to pick her up at the airport. With Daisy gone, I'd been incredibly productive. She didn't like me painting in the house because of the fumes, but since she was gone I figured what the hell. Creatively speaking, her absence was a breath of fresh air, and I'd gotten very involved in a new series of paintings exploring the dark side of popular cartoon characters, like Snoopy and Hello Kitty. When I paint I go into a sort of trance and lose track of time. Hell, she's lucky I heard the phone ring when she called me to come pick her up.

I got to the airport as quickly as I could, but it still took me over an hour because of all the road construction. She tossed her backpack in the trunk, then got in the car without saying a word. She didn't talk to me until we were blocks from home.

"I left my itinerary on the refrigerator door. I highlighted the date and time of my flight." She let out a gasp and slammed her right foot to the floor, like she was hitting the brakes from the passenger side.

"Watch it you moron!" I screamed as I swerved around a stopped city bus, nearly hitting a fluorescent green VW Beetle that was hiding in my blind spot in the process. "Sorry. I meant the bus driver, not you."

I reached over to put my hand on her knee, but she slapped it away. "Come on, Dais, if you're going to be mad at me, get mad for a good reason."

"Forgetting to pick me up isn't a good reason?" Her voice was venom; she hissed like a cobra.

"Not as good as this one: I accidentally killed your philodendron."

She took a sharp breath, then shook her head slowly. "How the hell do you kill a philodendron? They'll survive in a closet, for god's sake."

That was the defining moment. My marriage was over.[24]

Notice when I go into the flashback from novel-time (meaning, real time), I slip into the past-perfect tense in a few places to indicate I'm now in flashback. I wrote, I'd been incredibly productive....I'd gotten very involved... And while it is perfectly okay to do an entire flashback in past-perfect tense, notice that after the first few uses I slipped into simple past tense.

Flashbacks can be short—something as short as writing:

> I remember baking cookies with my grandmother over the winter holidays. Her kitchen always smelled of brown sugar and cinnamon.

Or flashbacks can take up entire chapters of books. The important thing to remember is, be sure your reader knows when you are going into flashback by using past-perfect tense, then be sure to bring the reader back to novel-time in a manner that makes it perfectly clear the flashback is over. In the above excerpt from *Breathe,* the line <That was the defining moment> indicates coming out of flashback.

SubPlots

Unless you're writing for young children, your novel will likely contain a main plot and **subplots**. Subplots are story lines that are outside of, yet somehow in the end tie into the main story line. Most novels have at least one subplot.

The main plot of *Redeeming Grace* revolves around Grace trying to save baby sister Miriam from their verbally and physically abusive father. The main subplot deals with Otto's anguish over keeping secret a tragedy he feels he caused years before he knew Grace, a tragedy that left one person dead and his brother forever changed. The stories are separate—the former deals with Grace and Miriam, the latter with Otto and Henry—but in the end, they tie together to bring the climax scene to its apex.

The trick with subplots is knowing where to disperse them throughout your novel. Some writer's will put one chapter of main plot, then a chapter of subplot, then a chapter of main plot, and so on throughout the novel.

That works fine if you have an equal number of main plot chapters and subplot chapters. But it can get predictable, and predictability isn't good in a novel. You want your readers to be surprised with every turn of the page.

Try mixing them up a little. Put two main plot chapters, then a subplot, then maybe one main plot and two subplots. Play around with them. You should be able to rearrange chapters from each plot line with a minimum of difficulty until you find a sequence that helps to build the suspense while keeping all plot lines fresh in the readers' minds. Try not to go more than three chapters without returning to your main plot line, however. If you go any longer than that, you risk confusing your readers.

What Scenes Should Accomplish

No matter how many plot lines your novel contains, no matter how many scenes make up your story, when writing always remember a scene should do at least two of the following things: **describe setting, advance your plot, develop the characters,** or **increase the suspense**.

How do you know if your scenes accomplish these goals?

A story should paint a picture with words, and a three-dimensional, color picture at that. If one of your goals in your scene is to **describe setting**, ask yourself, "When readers finished this scene, will they have a color picture of the setting fixed in their minds?" If the answer is 'yes', congratulations! You've achieved your goal.

Plot is what happens in your story. It's got nothing to do with your character's motives, or the theme of your story. Plot is simply the events that take place in the course of the tale.

If the purpose of your scene is to **advance the plot**, ask yourself, "What is the goal for the character's actions in this scene?" For example, your goal may be to reveal some childhood trauma to provide motivation for your character's current actions. Or, it may be to introduce the conflict in your story. If the character's actions achieve your goal, you have advanced your plot—the events of the story have moved forward.

Does your reader feel something for your character after reading the scene? It could be love, hate, or sympathy. If your words create a connection between reader and character, you're scene meets the criteria for **developing the characters.**

Does the scene pose a question to readers? Does it leave them wondering if the character can overcome childhood traumas in order to succeed at whatever it is they are trying to accomplish? Will the mystery be solved? Will they fall in love? If your scene poses a question in the readers minds, it has a **suspense focus**.

Scene/Sequel Theory

One of the basic laws of physics is, *for every action there is an equal and opposite reaction.* We all learned in high school about cause and effect, about stimulus-response (remember Pavlov's dogs?). You drop a ball, it falls to the ground. You go to work, you get paid. Someone sneezes in your face, you catch their cold. These are real-life examples of these scientific principles.

Fiction works the same way. Stories are a series of causes and their effects. This happens on both a large scale—Civil War breaks out (cause), Scarlett must learn a new way of life (effect)—and on a small scale—Character

X says something to Character Y (cause), and Character Y answers (effect).

Sometimes, the effect is immediate. Bill throws the ball (cause), Bob catches it (effect). But sometimes, the effect takes place later. Sometimes a cause happens, and before the effect can be known, the character must *internalize* the action, or cause, before the effect can be known.

For example, lets say you're writing a story about Mary and Tom and their marriage. Let's say Mary finds out Tom is having an affair with her best friend. This is a stimulus, or cause. Mary then takes off on a week-long retreat to mull over the mess her life has become and to figure out what to do. This is internalization. While on her retreat, she has an epiphany, returns home, divorces Tom, and moves to Tibet to become a Buddhist nun. This is the response, or effect.

When writing your story, keep in mind that every cause must have an effect, every stimulus must have a response. For every action, there must be an equal and opposite reaction—our basic law of physics.

These effects, these responses, are how you advance your plot. Plot—what happens in your story—is a series of cause and effects, of stimuli and responses.

This is sometimes known as **scene/sequel theory**. Your action (your cause) is the scene; the reaction (response) is the sequel. But this language can lead to confusion, since we've already learned scene to mean a building block of story. If you ever read something about scene/sequel theory, just remember our basic law of physics.

Every story asks a question. Will Scarlett be able to save Tara? Will Romeo and Juliet live happily ever after? Will Ahab get the whale? Each scene in your story—whether you are writing a 2,500-word short story, or a 200,000-word epic novel—should present a challenge to the characters resolving that question.

As the story unfolds, your characters come closer and closer to resolving the question. Sometimes they take two steps forward then one step back, but overall, they should make slow, steady progress toward conflict resolution.

When the story finally reaches its apex, its climax, the story question is resolved (either satisfactorily, as in the Scarlett and Tara example; or unsatisfactorily, as in the Romeo and Juliet example; In *Moby Dick* whether the question is resolved or not depends on whether you're rooting for Ahab or the whale).

Your climax, your apex, MUST be written in scene—scene meaning action, in this case. You don't want Character X telling Character Y about how they resolved their conflict. You don't want to tell it in flashback. The climax scene must be written in *novel time*, meaning in the now. It should be fast paced.

PACING

How does one set the pace for a story? And how do you know what the proper pace is for each scene you write?

Use **normal pace** when the story is progressing, but nothing special is happening. Normal pace is used for setting description, as a segue between two or more dramatic scenes, and/or to give readers a break from the action, allowing you to tone down the pace so you can build it up again.

Create normal pace by using an even blend of description, dialogue, and narration.

Use **fast pace** when the story needs to shift to a higher gear; for example, during an action scene or when your characters are engaged in an emotional confrontation.

Create fast pace by focusing on only one fictional element to the near exclusion of all others. For example, use only dialogue, or only narration of action. Fast pace is created with short, concise sentences, not long winded prose.

Use **atmospheric pace** to create a mood or a specific feeling. Atmospheric pace is used for setting a romantic scene, for example, or to create gloom or melancholy.

Create atmospheric pace by blending physical and psychological description to set the mood you want your readers to experience.

Use **suspenseful pace** to keep the readers on the edge of their seats. Suspenseful pace is frequently used in mysteries, for example.

Create suspenseful pace by focusing on step-by-step detail and action that work toward, but delay, the ultimate payoff.

The best novels are a compilation of scenes told at different paces. You'll have an atmospheric paragraph or two, which segue into a scene that is normal pace. Then, the tension kicks up a notch or two until you're writing at a suspenseful pace, which builds and builds until you're breathless from the fast paced action flying from your fingertips and into your computer.

Putting It All Together

How do you put your scenes together to build your story? The best stories are compilations of scenes where your protagonist strives to overcome obstacles thrown in his or her way in order to achieve a goal. Remember, it isn't always a lofty goal—the goals can be quite modest. The size of the goal isn't important. What is important is how badly your character wishes to achieve the goal.

Let's look at a familiar fairy tale. In *Snow White*, the main character's goal is finding true love. The story's conflicts include an evil stepmother, a hunter who drags her into the woods to kill her, a bunch of dwarves that want to keep her as their own personal handmaid, and that dreadful poisoned apple. (One might argue Snow's inability to stand up for herself and her gullibility are also conflicts—after all, she follows the hunter willingly, keeps the dwarves tidy with no complaint, and allows an ugly hag to convince her to bite into the apple.) Each of these challenges is presented in a new scene. And in each scene, Snow either figures out a way to deal with the challenge (like convincing the hunter not to kill her), or the challenge gets the best of her (she took a bite into the apple). In the end, the prince rides up, kisses and awakens her, and she rides off into the sunset with her true love, conflict resolved.

Personally, I'd like to see more fairy tales where the princess takes charge of her own destiny and doesn't depend on the prince to do the saving—but that's not the point. The point is, once the conflict is resolved, the story concludes.

Exercises

1. Write a scene that contains a flashback.
2. Write a scene that is fast paced.

Chapter Seven

The End

So, at last, your story question is resolved, Snow White has her prince; Romeo and Juliet are dead. (Remember, not all conflicts are resolved happily.) How do you end your story?

The resolution of the conflict—the climax—is not the end. You're close, but you're not quite there yet. At this point, you must decide whether your story is going to have a *closed-ending* or an *open-ending*.

In an **closed-ending** story, the ending is where your character, your reader, or sometimes both, learn the consequences of the dramatic series of events that transpired during the course of the story. It's called the *denouement*, which roughly translated means "untying the knot." In a novel, the denouement is usually the final chapter, although at times it may be longer.

Let's take a final look at Flannery O'Connor's *A Good Man is Hard to Find.* The last excerpt we read found the grandmother and her family face to face with The Misfit, an escaped convict. Throughout the story, The Misfit's men, Hiram and Bobby Lee, have taken the family members, a few at a time, deep into the woods. Gunshots follow; Hiram and Bobby Lee return alone. The grandmother is frantically trying to convince The Misfit he isn't all bad; that he must have some good in him somewhere. Here's the climax of the story:

> ...She saw the man's face twisted close to her own as if he were going to cry and she murmured, "Why you're one of my babies. You're one of my own children!" She reached out and touched him on the shoulder. The Misfit sprang back as if a snake had bitten him and shot her three times through the chest. Then he put his gun down on the ground and took off his glasses and began to clean them.[25]

Conflict resolved. Not prettily—the grandmother, her son and his wife, and her grandchildren are all dead. But the conflict is resolved.

Denouement follows:

Hiram and Bobby Lee returned from the woods and stood over the ditch, looking down at the grandmother who half sat and half lay in a puddle of blood with her legs crossed under her like a child's and her face smiling up at the cloudless sky.

Without his glasses, The Misfit's eyes were red-rimmed and pale and defenseless-looking. "Take her off and thow her where you thown the others," he said, picking up the cat that was rubbing itself against his leg.

"She was a talker, wasn't she?" Bobby Lee said, sliding down the ditch with a yodel.

"She would have been a good woman," The Misfit said, "if it had been somebody there to shoot her every minute of her life."

"Some fun!" Bobby Lee said.

"Shut up, Bobby Lee," The Misfit said. "It's no real pleasure in life."[26]

O'Connor chooses to use *poignant dialogue* in her denouement. With this technique, dialogue reveals something about the characters: what they are afraid of, for example, or how they've changed from the events of the story.

Does The Misfit's last sentences indicate he's learned something, or changed, from his encounter with the grandmother?

But poignant dialogue isn't the only way to end a story. Eudora Welty chooses to use *poignant description* at the end of her story about a woman waiting for the lover who left her years earlier, *At the Landing*:

> The old woman nodded, and nodded out to the flowing river, with the firelight following her face and showing its dignity. The younger boys separated and took their turns throwing knives with a dull *pit* at the tree.[27]

A simple description, a woman looking at the river, boys throwing knives at a tree. But the simplicity is a metaphor for the woman and her lost love, the love that has passed as surely as the water in the river flows by; the knives hitting the tree with a dull *pit* akin to the pain in her heart.

Climax resolution; denouement. The closed-ending story ends.

Sometimes, stories have an **open ending**. With an open-ended story, the story ends before the conflict is resolved, leaving the reader to wonder, "Did she or didn't she?"

Truman Capote's story *Miriam* is an example of an open-ended story. Miriam is a young girl of about ten who is stalking a widow, Mrs. H.T. Miller (whose first name also happens to be Miriam). The widow is terrified of the little girl.

As the story draws near the end, Miriam brings a box of clothes to the widow's apartment and announces she is moving in. The widow runs to a neighbor's apartment for help. The neighbor goes to the widow's apartment, but quickly returns and insists no one is there. Shaken, the widow returns to her home.

The story ends as follows:

As though moving in a dream, she sank to a chair. The room was losing shape; it was dark and getting darker and there was nothing to be done about it; she could not lift her hand to light a lamp.

Suddenly, closing her eyes, she felt an upward surge, like a diver emerging from some deeper, greener depth. In times of terror or immense distress, there are moments when the mind waits, as though for a revelation, while a skein of calm is woven over thought; it is like a sleep, or a supernatural trance; and during this lull one is aware of a force of quiet reasoning: well, what if she had never really known a girl named Miriam? that she had been foolishly frightened on the street? In the end, like everything else, it was of no importance. For the only thing she had lost to Miriam was her identity, but now she knew she had found again the person who lived in this room, who cooked her own meals, who owned a canary, who was someone she could trust and believe in: Mrs. H.T. Miller.

Listening in contentment, she became aware of a double sound: a bureau drawer opening and closing: she seemed to hear it long after completion—opening and closing. Then gradually, the harshness of it was replaced by the murmur of a silk dress and this, delicately fain, was moving nearer and swelling in intensity till the walls trembled with the vibration and the room was caving under a wave of whispers. Mrs. Miller stiffened and opened her eyes to a dull, direct stare.

"Hello," said Miriam.[28]

Has Miriam really returned to terrorize Mrs. Miller? Was there ever really a Miriam, or has she always been a figment of the widow's imagination? Or, was she real, but her return only a dream? Readers must draw their own conclusions, for Capote leaves us with only the questions, not the answers. The story is open-ended.

Whether you chose an open-ending or a closed-ending, the most important thing about the end of a story is that **when you reach the end, stop writing**! That may sound like a no-brainer, but it never ceases to amaze me how difficult a time some writers have ending their stories.

Stories are not high school themes. There is no thesis statement that needs to be summarized at the end. You don't need to summarize your story.

One of the best ways to determine what you last sentence should be is to delete your last line. Does the ending still make sense? Does it have power? If your answer is 'yes', delete the new last sentence, and ask yourself the same questions. Continue doing this until you reach the point where if you delete the sentence, the ending no longer makes sense and no longer has power. This should be the last sentence in your story.

Exercise

Write a scene that begins with the dialogue sentence, "Put down that telephone!" and ends with the line, <In the end, it didn't really matter, because she ran off anyway.>

114

CHAPTER EIGHT

FALLOW TIMES:

DEALING WITH WRITER'S BLOCK

If there is anything a writer fears more than a crashed hard drive, it's writer's block. The terror of one day sitting down, poising our fingers over the keyboard, and nothing coming out is enough to send most writers back to bed.

As I am writing this chapter, I'm sitting at my desk, which sits smack-dab in the center of my living room window, overlooking my back yard. It is early March. Last year this time, I looked out on crocus blooming and hyacinth poking through the warming soil. Today, I look out on six inches of newly fallen snow and grumpy squirrels who are having to dig to find the corn I threw out for them last night.

Writing can be like weather. Sometimes, ideas spring through the fertile soil of your mind and blossom on the page with what seems like little effort at all. Other times, you can sit at the computer for hours and, dig as you might, not be able to find an idea for all the snowdrifts.

This is okay. In fact, it's a necessary part of being a writer. I don't believe in writer's block. When we can't tap our ideas, it doesn't mean we don't have any. It means they aren't ripe yet; they aren't ready for birth. Any organic gardener will tell you fallow times are just as crucial to a good harvest as growing times. The soil needs to rest, to prepare itself for the next growing season. Your creative imagination is exactly the same. It needs to lie fallow and rest between crops of good stories. Winter of the mind is as crucial to a story as winter of the earth is to a good harvest.

That's all very well and good, you may be thinking, but what if I've been in a fallow time for too long? How can I jump start my ideas?

Different methods work for different people. What one writer swears is the cure for writer's block, another writer will say doesn't help at all. This list of suggestions is just that—a list of suggestions. If one trick doesn't work for you, try another.

- *Change your routine.* I'm a morning person. I can happily awaken at 5:00 A.M., fix a cup of coffee, and write until noon. Then, at exactly 12:02 P.M., my brain turns to mush and I can't write any longer. I have writer friends whose schedules are just the opposite. They sleep until noon and write into the wee hours of the night. If you're blocked, shake up your routine. Try writing in the morning if you're a night owl, or writing at night if you're like me, a morning person.

- *Write something different.* Yes, you're working on your Great American Novel. But if you're blocked, you aren't working on it, are you? Try writing a poem, a limerick, haiku. Write a love letter to your partner. Write a song. Don't worry if it's good or not. Good isn't the issue—writing is. It's very possible that the simple act of putting pen to paper (or keystroke to keyboard) is all you'll need to jump start your creative imagination.

- *Take a walk.* Or, go to the gym. Play tennis, or golf. Sometimes our brains don't work because we've spent so many hours hunched over our computers our bodies are turning into piles of mashed potatoes. A little exercise will lift your spirits, tone your body, and give your creativity a jolt.

- *Play with toys.* Yup, toys. I hereby give you permission to put playthings on your desk. If you don't have any toys, go to the store and buy some. The reasoning behind this is quite simple. Think for a moment: who are the most creative people you know? Children, of course. Remember as a child casting aside your newly unwrapped holiday presents to turn the box into a spaceship? How many of you made forts from your parents' dining room chairs? Playing with toys will bring out your inner child. Your creative, inner child.

- *Practice some other creative art.* This is similar to the toy thing, and works well for people who are so grown up they can't find their inner child anymore. (But that isn't you, is it? I didn't think so.) Your creative nature is like your health. It needs to be fed and nurtured. Carrots are a healthy food, but your body wouldn't stay healthy for very long if you ate only carrots, would it? The same is true for your creative nature. Feed it only one food—fiction writing, in most of our cases—and that creative nature will grow unhealthy. To keep it fit, sculpt clay, paint with watercolors, or take up jewelry making. Make a collage. It doesn't matter what it is, just so long as it is new to you and creative. It doesn't have to be very good; no one has to see it but you. I am partial to making little statues and figurines out of Sculpey clay, and to making jewelry from semi-precious stones. But sometimes I dabble in watercolors, silk dyeing, and book making. Every time I finish an art project, I feel like I can return to my computer and take on the world.

- *Go ahead and write crap.* If you really, truly don't want to do anything other than work on your novel, by all means, sit at your computer and write crap. It is easier to fix bad writing than it is to create something from nothing. It could be that writing crap will wake up your muse enough to make her indignant and come rushing back to help you dig yourself out of that big pile.

CHAPTER NINE

REVISION

Congratulations, you've finished your story! You're now ready to send your baby out into the world, to try to get it published.

Or are you?

The truth is, probably not. What you have just completed is the first draft of a story, not a final draft. Almost without exception, first drafts must go through revisions before you have truly reached The End.

Revising can be intimidating, because there are so many things you have to look at. The key to successfully revising your manuscript is to compartmentalize your approach. Instead of trying to revise all aspects of the story at once, concentrate on only one element at a time. The advantage to doing this is your attention is fully focused on that one area alone; you aren't distracted from your goal by other problems.

For example, if you are revising dialogue and run across a problematic narrative passage, don't fix it right then. Flag it, and come back to it when you are revising narrative. I find getting mini-Post-It notes in different colors is a good way to do this. I use one color notes for dialogue, one for grammar and structure, and yet another for characterization, for example.

Plot Structure

We'll start here, because your plot is the armature that holds your story together. Once your armature is aligned properly, putting the rest of the pieces in place is much easier.

What you are looking for here is that the plot events are in the right order, and that your story builds to a satisfactory climax. Scene/sequel, action/reaction, stimulus/response, each scene building upon the last until you reach your climax.

Here is where you should examine each scene and ensure it accomplishes as least two things: describe setting, advance your plot, develop the characters, or increase the suspense.

Think of each scene as being a mini-story: it has a beginning, middle, and end. The beginning introduces the conflict of the scene, the middle complicates it, and the ending resolves it. That means each scene should have a hot spot, a point where the action and or emotion reaches an apex. Usually, your scene builds toward this. When revising for structure, make sure you locate the hot spot, and make sure it generates enough heat to justify the scene's existence in your story. If you can't find a hot spot—for example, if you make the common error of wanting to write pages and pages of background to "set the scene"—then you need to rethink your scene.

Texture

When looking at your story's texture, your goal is to sharpen descriptive passages to make your characters, setting, and action more vivid.

Begin by looking for **too much** or **too little description**. Jean Auel, author of the *Clan of the Cave Bear* series of epic novels, is famous for her over-description of setting. Especially in her most recent book of the series, *The Shelters of Stone*, she goes on for page after page of detailed description of the plant life in paleo-Europe. This is fine for Jean Auel, who sells millions of books and makes her publisher millions of dollars. This is not fine for the rest of us, however. Too much description bogs down a story. You are in danger of losing your readers with too much description, because they get bored. There are too many good stories out there for your average reader to have the patience to finish a story that bogs down.

By the same token, too little description leaves the reader wondering where the action is taking place; what the setting looks like. Remember, your words should paint a color, three-dimensional picture of setting. Use specifics, not generalities. For example, look at this sentence:

The truck went down the street.

I'd bet my last dollar every one of you formed a different picture in your head from that sentence. What kind of truck are we talking about? There's a world of difference between an eighteen-wheeler and a 1942 Dodge. How does the narrator know the truck went down the street? Did he hear it? See it? Smell its exhaust? Did the house shake?

As you are looking at your descriptions, ensuring your words paint color pictures, look out for **clichéd word choices**. Certain words and phrases have been done to death. (Whoops! 'Done to death' is one of them!) A woman tossing her long, blonde hair; a man with a chiseled jaw; describing eyes as cornflower blue, and a heart skipping a beat at the sight of a lover are just a few examples of images that are old, tired, and cliché.

The problem is, writers love to use these descriptions because they make sense. They bring a clear, vivid picture to mind. But editors hate them, because they aren't fresh or exciting. Clichés do not belong in your story.

Next, look at your **adjectives and adverbs**. With modifiers, the rule is: less is more. This is especially true of adverbs, particularly adverbs ending in 'ly'. Why? Because most of the time, adverbs are an indication you've used a weak verb, and weak verbs are a sure sign of weak writing. For example, you've written this sentence:

She walked quietly across the floor and gently shut the door.

You have two verbs here, *walked* and *shut*. Each one is modified by an adverb, *quietly* and *gently*. The two verbs are weak verbs. What do we mean by *walked*? What do we mean by *shut*? What if, instead, you wrote:

She tiptoed across the floor and eased the door shut.

Much better! You still have two verbs, but *tiptoed* is a stronger, meaning more descriptive, verb than *walked*, and you've eliminated *shut* as a verb completely (and, in fact, turned it into an adjective modifying the word *door*), replacing it with the stronger verb *eased*.

Pay particular attention to adverb use in tag lines. Characters who *said happily*, *replied angrily*, or *exclaimed merrily* can make them sound like they've got some strange caffeine buzz. If you have to use an adverb in your tag line, go back and look at the line of dialogue. Strengthen the line in order to convey the happiness, anger, or merriment, and eliminate the adverb from the tag line. Here are some examples:

1. "I got an A on my chemistry test," Lizzie said happily.

    " I'm so excited—I got an A on my chemistry test!" Lizzie said.

2. "The dog died," Sam said sadly.

    Sam was so choked with tears he stuttered as he whispered, "The d-d-dog died."

Dialogue

The goal of dialogue is to elicit character personality through conversation. Weak dialogue will sink your story quickly, because it makes your characters one dimensional and unbelievable.

Begin by examining your **tag lines**. Are they in the right place? Remember, if you need to use a tag line, put it in as soon as is stylistically possible.

Emerging writers have a tendency to use too many tag lines. Use a tag line of some sort at the beginning of each bit of dialogue so we know who is speaking. After that, use them sparingly, or not at all if the dialogue is between only two characters. You'll need to use tag lines more frequently in dialogue where more than two characters are speaking, of course. Use a tag line whenever you need one to avoid reader confusion.

Remember to keep tag lines simple. The simpler, the better, in fact. *He said* or *Julie said* is far better than having your characters stating, exclaiming, replying, querying, retorting, and proclaiming. If you find yourself using this sort of tag line, go back and strengthen the line of dialogue so you can *show* us this is what the character is doing, rather than having to *tell* us. Remember the rule: Show, don't tell.

Look for **bland or melodramatic lines**. Always ask yourself, "Is this bit of dialogue compelling?" For dialogue *must* be compelling. Leave out the boring parts. We know when two characters meet on the street, they're going to exchange pleasantries before getting into the meat of their conversation. You don't need to put the pleasantries in as dialogue—they aren't compelling.

Editing

The goal here is to ensure your manuscript is clear, correct, and concise.

First, is it **clear**? Do you use words and phrases that are familiar to the reader? It's okay to use an unfamiliar word occasionally, especially if that word's meaning becomes clear within the context of the sentence. But to use long, unusual words just for the sake of using them is showing off, not good writing. I once read a story in *The New Yorker* where the author used the word 'inchoate' five times in a 3,500 word story! That was four times too many for an unusual adjective. (I was writing *The Cabin* at the time. This overuse of a word irked me so much that when I next sat down to write, I intentionally threw in one "inchoate shadow". I felt a tremendous satisfaction doing that; I don't know why!)

Be sure your words are specific rather than general. Remember the truck going down the street? Say eighteen-wheeler if that's what you mean; say maple rather than just tree, pigeon rather than bird, cocker spaniel rather than dog. Specifics, once again, help transform a black-and-white image into color.

Next, is your manuscript **correct**? Is it punctuated correctly? Remember, each sentence must have terminal punctuation. Use the simplest piece of punctuation possible—never use an exclamation point if a period will do, for example. Use strong verbs to indicate someone is exclaiming, not exclamation points.

Know when to use a comma, semicolon, or colon. Overuse of semicolons is one of the biggest punctuation errors I see. If you are uncertain what punctuation to use where, pick up a style guide, like Strunk and White's or the *Chicago Manual of Style*.

In dialogue, the terminal punctuation goes inside the close-quotation mark. Occasionally, you will see a story or book where the punctuation is outside the close-quotation mark. This is how it is done in Europe. In America, it goes inside the close-quotation mark. Always.

Hyphenate adjective if they come before the word they modify, but not after. For example, look at the sentence:

I used six inch nails.

Did I use six nails that were an inch long, or nails that were six inches long? Assuming we mean the latter, the sentence should read:

I used six-inch nails,
OR
I used nails that were six inches long.

Next, look at spelling. Don't rely on your computer's spell checker to do this for you. If you misspell *where* as *wear*, your spell checker won't catch the error. Read what you've written. Better yet, have someone else read it. Writers are notorious for easily spotting errors in other people's writing, but not being able to find their own mistakes. This is because when we've written something, we see what it is *supposed* to say and not what we may have actually written.

Watch out for troublesome twins, or homophones. These are words that sound alike but are spelled differently. If you aren't sure which word to use, look it up in the dictionary.

Look for errors in syntax. Syntax is the way we arrange our words in order to convey meaning. Often when we speak, our syntax is garbled, but those listening to us still understand our meaning. When we write, we have to be sure our syntax is correct.

For example, look at this sentence:

> If you toddler will not drink cold milk, put it in the microwave for a few moments.

Put what in the microwave? There is a choice of antecedents here. Pity the poor toddler if the caregiver makes the wrong choice here!

Here's another example of a syntax error:

> Do you ride the bus or carry a briefcase?

This is what is called a ***non sequitur***, which roughly translated means 'nonsense'. And it is just that— what does riding the bus have to do with carrying a briefcase?

One of the biggest syntax errors writers make is placing the word *only* in the wrong place. For example:

> Due to the high cost of gasoline, we can only pump ten gallons of fuel per customer.

'Only' is in the wrong place. The sentence is saying that whoever 'we' is can only pump ten gallons of fuel. They cannot eat, breath, or walk and chew gum at the same time. They can only pump fuel. To be correct, the sentence should read:

> Due to the high cost of gasoline, we can pump only ten gallons of fuel per customer.

Another word to look for is *that*. If my editing projects are any indication, *that* is the most overused word in the English language. Smoky's ***rule of that*** is, if you can delete it and the sentence still makes sense, then you don't need it.

For example:

> I know that spring will be here soon.

Does the sentence make sense if you remove *that*? Let's see:

> I know spring will be here soon.

Yes, the sentence makes sense. Delete *that.*

Finally, is your story **concise**? There are several things you want to look at to ensure your story is as tight as possible.

First, look for subplots that go nowhere, or characters that don't belong in the story. I remember an episode of the television show *ER* where early in the show, a patient is shown turning up tarot cards on a tray by her bed. A nurse asks her about it, and the tarot lady tells her to come back later and she'll read the nurse's cards. But they never show the tarot lady again, leaving viewers to wonder why she was there in the first place. It could have been an interesting subplot, but they dropped the ball. Make sure you don't have any tarot ladies in your stories.

Looking for conciseness also means once again examining your modifiers. Yes, you want to be specific in your descriptions, but you've gone too far if you feel compelled to write:

A red 1978 Dodge pickup with "Joe's Gourmet Mushrooms and Vacuum Repair" stenciled on the side, pink panther mud flaps, a dent in the front left fender, and broken right rear tail light went down the road.

Remember, less is more. In this case, unless something about the truck is pertinent to the story (for example, you're writing a murder mystery and a witness remembered only that the getaway truck had pink panther mud flaps), saying <a red Dodge pickup truck> is probably just fine. If in doubt, follow the *rule of three*: use no more than three modifiers in your descriptions.

Finally, don't forget to get a little help from your friends. Show your story to as many qualified people as possible. By qualified, I mean people who read a lot and, if possible, people who write. Showing it to other people means they will give you opinions, and that's the point.

Many writers go ballistic when they get their story back and the person offers suggestions. What the writer really wanted was someone to say, "It's perfect. The most moving/funny/life-altering story I've ever read. Don't change a thing." I can tell you right now, unless the person you've shown the story to is your mother—whose job description requires her to think everything you write is worthy of a Pulitzer Prize—this isn't going to happen. Instead of resisting editorial advice, examine it as objectively as possible. If the advice makes sense, use it. If it doesn't ignore it. But be open to it.

I show all my work to my good friend Kat, who, like me, works as a freelance editor. When she gives me her critique, I sometimes want to shout at her, "What's wrong with you? Can't you recognize literary genius when you see it? What kind of dopey, idiotic suggestions are these?" And so on and so forth. There's a fight scene in my novel, *Redeeming Grace*, where one character has his glasses broken. Kat made me stand up and walk through the fight scene, blow by blow, with her, to ensure the glasses could indeed have broken in the manner I described. (They could have...phew!)

No matter what her comments, I eventually take the list, read it over, think about it, and change whatever I agree with, which usually is somewhere between eighty and ninety percent of what she suggested. Every story, every chapter of my novels, Kathi has critiqued, and every one is significantly improved by her suggestions.

Many communities have writing groups you can join to get this sort of feedback. Churches, book stores, and community colleges are all placed you can look for writing groups. If you can't find one, start one. Don't ignore the Internet. There are writing groups there, too, for every genre.

Exercises

Rewrite the following sentences using descriptive language:

1. It was a dark and stormy night.

2. A truck passed.

3. Over the meadow and through the woods to grandmother's house we go.

Edit the following sentences for syntax:

1. "If Sam's not coming home for supper, I only want a sandwich," Jan said.

2. She likes going to the ballet, playing tennis, and to read books.

3. Broken into a thousand pieces, the bull just snorted and paid no attention to the once-priceless china that littered the shop floor.

4. The top prize of two million dollars went to George Smith, a tall, muscular man with a red birthmark on his left cheek.

5. Do you play golf once a week or eat lunch at your desk?

6. Running along the lakefront in downtown Chicago, a tall ship caught my eye.

7. He talked about his twenty years on death row for a murder he did not commit with the local news media.

Rewrite these tired clichés with fresh images:

1. His heart turned to stone.

2.   He gazed into the pools of her cornflower blue eyes.

3.   She was pretty as a picture.

4.   He was strong as an ox.

6.   It was hotter than hell.

7.   I'd move heaven and earth to have you back again.

Edit the following for punctuation:

1.   Rose went out into the garden "Its cold out here" she said.

2.   "When will we get there?" he thought.

3.   "Could you pass me the buttermilk"? Sally asked.

4.   She said Brad was the only man for her.

Which sentence has the more-correct meaning:

1.   Good girls don't go to dirty movie theaters.

                    OR

Good girls don't go to dirty-movie theaters.

2.   I saw a man eating lobster.

                    OR

I saw a man-eating lobster.

Circle the correct word:

1.   The smell of pot roast really (**wet/whet**) my appetite.

2.   I'm not feeling well; I want to (**lay/lie**) down.

3. We were (all ready/ already) to go.

4. Sherry (**complimented/complemented**) the chef on how well the sauce (**complimented/ complemented**) the soufflé.

5. I went to the office supply store to buy some (**stationary/stationery**) and envelopes.

6. (**It's/ Its**) not fair that she gets to go and I don't.

7. His (**conscience/conscious**) set the remorseful thief apart from the defiant one.

8. She was (**anxious/eager**) to collect her lottery winnings.

9. The kids (**snuck/sneaked**) into the school through the back door but were caught by the (**principal/ principle.**)

Chapter Ten

Submitting Your Work

Agent or Publisher?

The time has come. This time, you really, truly are ready to submit your work. Now what?

The first thing you need to do is decide whether you want to use a literary agent or attempt to find a publisher on your own. While some authors swear you need to use an agent and while I have used one in the past, it isn't always necessary, and sometimes only costs you money. Most of the large presses require submission be through agents only, while many small presses prefer dealing directly with authors, leaving out the middle man.

Whether you want to try to sign with an agent or go directly to the publishers themselves, the steps are similar. First, you need to do your research.

Most literary agents handle certain types of books. Most publishers do the same. You don't want to submit your mystery thriller to an agent or publisher who handles only romance novels, or one who handles non-fiction only. All reputable literary agent and publishers have websites. Check them out and see what type of book they handle before making any queries.

A good place to look for an agent is the acknowledgement section of a book you love that is written in a similar vein as yours. Many authors name their agents there. You can also type "literary agent" into any online search engine and find agent websites.

To find a publisher, look at the front matter of similar books already in print. For first time authors, small, independent presses are your best bet. Again, insert "independent publishers" into your favorite search engine and you'll find links to their websites.

Once you've found a publisher you think would be a good fit for your novel, study their **submission guidelines.** These will be listed on virtually all publisher websites. Follow these guidelines carefully. If the guideline asks for a query letter and one-page synopsis (summary), send only that. If they ask for a synopsis and the first three chapters, send only that. If they ask for hard copy submissions only, don't presume it is okay to email them your submission. It isn't.

Query Letters

One thing you always will need when making a submission is a query letter. (If you study the submission guidelines—and I know you have—you'll find some publishers want only a query letter!). Your query letter should be crafted with as much care as your novel itself, because this is the first example of your writing a publisher will see. Mess up your query letter and your manuscript won't even be given a glance.

Open your query with a short teaser about your novel. Take a look at the back cover or front flap of any book in your library where the story is described. This is the sort of thing you are looking for—just enough information about the story to make the reader want to read more. Then, if you have any writing experience, say a few words about that. Include any other relevant information as well. For example, if you have a degree in ancient Roman history and your novel is set in ancient Rome, mention your expertise. If your novel is set in some exotic foreign land and you lived there for a year, mention that. This type of information gives your novel credibility.

Here is the query letter I used when I sent my novel *The Cabin* out into the world:

SMOKY TRUDEAU
123 Anystreet
Anywhere, US 12345

March 23, 3006

Ms. Jane Doe
GeeWhiz Publishing Co.
5432 Main Street
Some City, USA 55555

Dear Ms. Doe:

James-Cyrus Hoffmann has just inherited his grandfather's farm, and with it a mysterious cabin deep in the woods on Hoffmann mountain; a cabin he has dreamed about since childhood. When James-Cyrus enters the cabin, he is vaulted back through time to the Civil War era, where he meets Elizabeth, the brave young woman who lives in the cabin, and Malachi, a runaway slave. James-Cyrus realizes his dreams of the cabin were visions of the past, and that Elizabeth is his great-great aunt—a woman who vanished without a trace from the family tree. He also learns of his ancestors' pivotal role in the lives of dozens of runaway slaves who were offered a safe haven at the cabin, a station on the underground railroad.

Cora Spellmacher, James-Cyrus's elderly friend and neighbor, also has a window to the past, an ancient cauldron through which she can see Elizabeth. Cora begins to unravel the puzzle of how James-Cyrus is able to make his fantastic leaps back and forth through time. In doing so, Cora begins to hope a tragic wrong from her own past can be righted, and that she can regain something precious that was lost to her many years earlier.

Through his dreams and her observations in the cauldron, James-Cyrus and Cora come to realize Elizabeth and Malachi are in terrible danger. James-Cyrus and Cora then undertake a daring rescue mission that, if it succeeds, will rewrite the Hoffmann family history.

My first novel, *Redeeming Grace*, was published in 2004. I also have published a collection of short stories, co-authored a poetry chapbook, and am a Pushcart Prize nominee. When I'm not writing, I teach writing workshops at Parkland Community College and online.

I have enclosed the first chapter of *The Cabin* as well as a SASE for your response. I appreciate your time.

Sincerely yours,

Notice I jumped right into the short teaser about the novel. I didn't start out with a lot of pleasantries, no "How are you?" or "GeeWhiz Publishing Company looks like a perfect match for my novel." Publishers are busy people; they get dozens, even hundreds, of manuscripts every week. They don't want to have to wade through a bunch of pleasantries to get to the meat of the letter, and they obviously know you think your book is right for them or you wouldn't be sending submitting it to begin with.

Look at the fourth paragraph. Here, I outline my qualifications as a writer. Notice I don't list every short story, every poem, every feature article I've ever written. I stick with the highlights.

What if you have no writing experience? That's perfectly okay. Everyone has to get started at some point. Even prolific authors like Terry Pratchett and Stephen King had their first story. However, if you don't have any publishing credentials, don't draw attention to that fact. If *The Cabin* had been my first book, if I didn't have teaching credentials, I would simply not have written that fourth paragraph.

Look now at paragraph five of the letter. In it I say I've attached the first chapter of my novel and an SASE (self-addressed stamped envelope). At this point I would have looked up GeeWhiz Publishing on the Web and found that this is what they want—the first chapter. I didn't include a synopsis because they didn't ask for one, nor did I include more chapters than requested.

As far as the SASE goes, always include one with hard-copy submissions. Chances are, if your manuscript is purchased, you'll be notified by email or even a phone call. But send it anyway. If your manuscript is rejected, you have a better chance of finding out if you've given them the means to respond to you without it costing them anything. There's no need to send an envelope big enough for the return of your submission. A regular business envelope with first-class postage is all you need.

I'm often asked by students if it is okay to submit your manuscript to more than one publisher at a time. This is fine. It can take six months or longer for a publisher to respond to a query (and some never bother to reply at all, even with a SASE). However, keep careful records of where you send your queries. If you find a publisher, send the others a short note saying simply "I am withdrawing my manuscript, *My Book,* from consideration. Thank you." Put your book title in, of course—don't write *My Book.*

Chapter Eleven

Really Stupid Things Authors do to Screw Themselves

Chances are, you invested months, if not years, writing your novel. You've ignored your friends and family. Your dog hasn't gone for a romp in the park since you typed your first words.

With all that time and effort involved you don't want to do anything that will risk your book being published. Yet authors do exactly that by making breaches of etiquette, being greedy, and lacking common sense.

Let's start with your book itself.

Really Stupid Thing #1: Assuming Because Your Book is Fiction, You Can Change Facts and Pretend They're Real: I touched on this a bit in the first chapter, but it bears repeating: just because a book is fiction doesn't mean you can make up things and call them true. When the plot of your novel asks the question,

"What if things were different?" it is okay to rewrite history, or change a cultural belief. If your novel is a science fiction thriller where the earth has two moons, one of which is covered in a vast ocean, that's fine. But don't put a two-mooned earth in an historical novel about the Korean Conflict. Similarly, if the premise of your book is that men get pregnant and women don't, by all means, make your fellows pregnant. But don't put them in a traditional romance novel. Don't have Hindus eating beef, Jews worshiping to Vishnu, or Japan nuking the USA during World War II unless the premise of your novel is "What if?"

Really Stupid Thing #2: Forgetting What You've Already Written: When I wrote *Redeeming Grace,* I named Luther's church Brothers of the Holy Word. Later in the book, I referred to it as Brothers of the Bible church. Fortunately, my editor caught the mistake (thank you, Kat!). But it was a stupid mistake, and one I would not have made had I taken my own advice and consulted my characterization chart.

Similarly, I've seen Toyotas turn into Hondas, cocker spaniels turn into collies, and blonde hair turn brown (without benefit of hair dye).

Make a characterization chart. Consult it once in a while. You'll save yourself some embarrassment down the road.

Really Stupid Thing #3: Trusting Your Spell Checker: If ewe think yore spell checker will fined awl yore miss steaks, u r wrong.

Spell checkers are handy, and a useful place to start your proofread. But they're not infallible, as the above sentence makes clear. That sentence made it through my spell checker just fine.

Then again, you should never trust your own eyes to catch all your mistakes, either. Authors are notorious for being able to catch spelling errors in other writers' work, but not in their own. This is because the author sees what a sentence is *supposed* to say, not necessarily what it *does* say. It's always a good idea to have someone else read your manuscript before you submit it for publication.

Preferably someone you know can spell.

Really Stupid Thing #4: Assuming it is Okay to Have Typos and Punctuation Errors Because an Editor Will Fix Them: While it is true an editor will find and correct errors these and other errors, that's no reason to submit sloppy work. The fact is, if you can't be bothered to make sure your work is a technically perfect as possible before submitting it, the chances are the publisher will feel they can't be bothered working with you. This is a business where neatness counts.

Of course, no publisher expects a manuscript to be perfect. I can't remember the last time I read an actual published book (as opposed to a manuscript) where I didn't find at least one typo. We all make mistakes. But try to be as technically perfect as possible.

You've double-checked your manuscript, and you've corrected all your Really Stupid Things. The next thing you want to do is ensure you don't make any RST's in your submission.

Really Stupid Thing #5: Neglecting to proofread your query letter. One publisher I know got a query letter from an author who had obviously used the mail merge feature on his computer. Or, I should say, *tried* to use the mail merge feature. He goofed, and instead of his query letter going out saying "I am delighted to be submitting my novel for consideration to GeeWhiz Publishing Company"; it said "I am delighted to be submitting my novel for consideration to _____. In fact, there were three places in that letter where there was a big gaping void where the publishing company's name should have been.

An author I know told me her own embarrassing story. One independent press to which she submitted a query had already published a book authored by her friend. She mentioned this in her query letter. ("My friend, John Smith, author of *John Smith's Book*, suggested I write to you.") Unfortunately, she forgot to delete that opening sentence when she submitted the same query letter to three other publishing houses, none of whom had heard of John Smith or his book, and who could not have cared less that he referred her to them.

Proof read your query letter. Better yet, have someone else proof it for you.

Really Stupid Thing #6: Not Reading and Following the Publisher's Submission Guidelines. Publishers have guidelines for a reason: they feel their system is the best way for them to judge a manuscript's potential. But some authors take the word "guideline" literally, and think it is only that—a guideline.

Wrong. Perhaps the publishing industry should change the term *submission guidelines* to *submission requirements*, because that is a more accurate way to describe the package each publisher wants.

In addition to wanting a fascinating manuscript, publishers want to know their authors are willing and able to work with them, especially with their editors. This requires the ability to follow an editor's instructions. If you can't follow simple instructions on what to submit, why would a publisher have any reason to believe you'd be any better at following an editor's instructions?

Follow the instructions to the letter, even if they don't make sense to you. Otherwise, your submission will end up in the recycle bin faster than you can blink.

Really Stupid Thing #7: Admitting You Are Clueless. I've seen query letter where the author wrote, "I don't have any experience, but I think my book is very good and know you will too." Why would you admit you didn't have any experience? If your book is good, it won't matter. If your book is awful, it will matter even less. Never, ever give out negative information about yourself this way. If you consider yourself inexperienced, the publisher will, too. Also, don't presume to know a publisher will like your book. Of course, you hope they will. But you don't say that. You wouldn't be submitting your manuscript to them if you didn't think it was a good match.

Really Stupid Thing #8: Displaying an Over-Inflated Ego. You may think your YA fantasy novel is great, but that doesn't mean you write "My book is the next Harry Potter and will make me as famous as J.K. Rowling" in your query letter. Book critics decide whether you're the next Rowling, or Hemingway, or Faulkner—not authors.

Really Stupid Thing #9: Making Unrealistic Demands. My publisher once got a query letter where the author wrote, "I will require at least a $10,000 cash advance." Needless to say, that letter got pitched before the publisher got to the next sentence. Yes, some publishers offer cash advances. But certainly not all of them do, especially when you're talking about independent presses. Even when they do offer advances, they are likely to be a few hundred dollars, not thousands of dollars. This is especially true for unpublished authors. Advances are just that—advance payment of anticipated royalties. Publishers can't risk shelling out big bucks on an untried author and then not be able to recoup their losses.

Another author demanded her book be set in a certain type font and size, and formatted a certain way. These are publisher decisions, not author decisions. Publishers are experienced to know what type fonts look best for different types of books. Formatting is something that has to be done a particular way for the printer. If you are going to demand your book look a certain way, you're better off printing it yourself.

Some novice authors seem to think book tours are automatic things that publishers arrange. Book tours are nice, but once again, unless you're a high profile author with a history of writing best sellers, chances are if you want to do a book tour you're going to have arrange it yourself. Demanding your prospective publisher send you to Tahiti because your book is set there will give them a good laugh, but it won't get your book published.

Let's say you haven't made any of these mistakes, and your book has been picked up by a publisher.

Congratulations! But you aren't home free yet. There are still ways you can sabotage your story.

Really Stupid Thing #10: Not Cooperating with your Editor. Your manuscript will undoubtedly be edited before going to press. I make my living as an editor, and even my books get edited. This is a good thing. Editors are there to ensure your book is the very best book it can be. To quote my friend and fellow editor, Barbara Ardinger, Ph.D., "Editors make it so you won't embarrass yourself in print."

I once edited a book for a young woman whose book was rife with confusing terms, and the author refused to clarify them, saying readers should "look it up in the dictionary." She argued this point so much the publisher cancelled her contract. Now, instead of having a published book in her hands, she has only a confusing manuscript on her computer's hard drive.

Here are a few more sage suggestions from Barbara Ardinger:

Respect your editor. She's an expert in English grammar, punctuation, and usage. She knows how to fix a sentence whose subject and verb don't agree. She knows how to properly punctuate dialogue. She knows that not all the synonyms in the thesaurus are truly synonymous.

Don't sulk. Your editor is not trying to ruin your deathless prose. Even if you disagree with her and reject some of the changes she makes, look closely at the work she's doing to make your writing more accessible to your readers. Discuss issues with her so you can arrive at a compromise.

Answer the questions your editor asks you. Promptly. Your editor is trying to help you write a successful book, not write the book for you. She's probably not psychic. Just as your need her feedback, so does she need yours.

Do these examples and instructions mean you should never question your editor? Of course not! Recently I edited a book for an author whose original target audience were adults. I thought the book was much better suited for a YA audience, and told him he should make his characters younger to appeal to that market niche. We made a compromise: he made one character younger and left the other one older. It was a perfect idea, and his book is much stronger for having done so.

Really Stupid Thing #11: Expecting Your Publisher to do All Your Marketing For You: It's nice when a publisher goes all out to market your books. Most reputable ones do, sending review copies to appropriate venues, getting the books listed at the big distributing houses, and sending press releases to media outlets.

But don't sit back and expect the publisher to do all the work. You're expected to do your fair share, too.

Throw a book release party and invite everyone you know. Ask friends and family members who live in different parts of the country to throw them, too. Develop an author website. Research book fairs and arrange for a booth at suitable venues. Create a writer's blog. Offer to do a writing workshop at your local high school. Do a public reading at your library, or at a local coffee house. These are all things that can pay off handsomely in sales, but they are things you, the author, need to arrange.

BACK-WORD

Spring finally arrived. The snow is gone, the squirrels no longer need to dig through the snow to find their corn, and the daffodils finally bloomed. Soon the bright magenta blossoms on my crab apple tree will fade and be replaced with a brilliant green blanket of leaves. The fallow times are gone. Now is the season of plenty.

Just as each season must end, so too must each book. This is the end of mine. I hope by sharing my insights into writing, I have bolstered your confidence in your writing ability, that you have learned a thing or two, that you now are ready to write that novel.

You know you've got it in you. It's been lurking there all along.

ENDNOTES

1. Lee, Harper. *To Kill a Mockingbird.* New York: Warner Books, Inc., 1960.

2. Lee, Sarah Natalia. *Saving Amy.* Seattle: Vanilla Heart Publishing, 2008.

3. "Open Secrets," by Alice Munro. From *Open Secrets.* New York: Alfred A. Knopf, 1995.

4. Hegi, Ursula. *Stones from the River.* New York: Simon and Schuster, 1995.

5. Cather, Willa. *O Pioneers!* Copyright: 1913 by Willa Cather.

6. "Crazy in the Stir," by Chester B. Himes. Copyright 1934 by Chester B. Himes.

7. "A Good Man is Hard to Find," by Flannery O'Connor. From *A Good Man is Hard to Find and Other Stories* by Flannery O'Connor. Copyright

15. "Report on the Barnhouse Effect," by Kurt Vonnegut. From *Welcome to the Monkey House* by Kurt Vonnegut. Copyright 1950,1951, 1953, 1954, 1955, 1956, 1958, 1960, 1961, 1962, 1964, 1966, 1968 by Kurt Vonnegut. First published in *Colliers* magazine.

16. "Good-bye Emily Dickinson," by Smoky Trudeau. Copyright 2003 by Smoky Trudeau. First published in *Potpourri* magazine.

17. Nabakov, Vladimir. *Lolita.* Copyright 1955 by Vladimir Nabakov. Paris, France: Olympia Press, 1955.

18. Dickens, Charles. *A Christmas Carol.* Public domain.

19. McInerney, Jay. *Bright Lights, Big City.* New York: Vintage Books, 1984.

20. Martin, Steve. *Shopgirl.* New York: Hyperion Books, 2001.

21. "Miriam," by Truman Capote. From *A Tree of Night and Other Stories A Tree of Night and Other Stories* by Truman Capote. Copyright 1945 by Truman Capote.

22. "Big Two-Hearted River," by Ernest Hemingway. From *In Our Time* by Ernest Hemingway. New York: Charles Scribner's Sons, 1925.

23. "A Good Man is Hard to Find," by Flannery O'Connor. From *A Good Man is Hard to Find and Other Stories* by Flannery O'Connor. Copyright 1948, 1953, 1954, 1955 by Flannery O'Connor; renewed 1981, 1983 by Regina O'Connor; renewed 1976 by Mrs. Edward O'Connor.

24. "Breathe," by Smoky Trudeau. Copyright 2003 by Smoky Trudeau.

26. "A Good Man is Hard to Find," by Flannery O'Connor. From *A Good Man is Hard to Find and Other Stories* by Flannery O'Connor. Copyright 1948, 1953, 1954, 1955 by Flannery O'Connor; renewed 1981, 1983 by Regina O'Connor; renewed 1976 by Mrs. Edward O'Connor.

27. "At the Landing," by Eudora Welty. From *The Wide Net* by Eudora Welty. Copyright 1941, 1942, 1943, 1969, 1970, 1971 by Eudora Welty.

28. "Miriam," by Truman Capote. From *A Tree of Night and Other Stories A Tree of Night and Other Stories* by Truman Capote. Copyright 1945 by Truman Capote.

Recommended Reading

On The Craft of Writing

Creating Fiction, edited by Julie Checkoway, Story Press, 1999.

Mastering Point of View, by Sherri Szeman, Story Press, 2001.

On The Writing Life

Bird by Bird, by Anne Lamott, Anchor Books, 1994.

On Writing: A Memoir of the Craft, by Stephen King, Scribner, 2000.

References

The Chicago Manual of Style (15th Edition). Chicago: University of Chicago Press, 2001.

The Elements of Style, William Strunk and E.B. White. New York: MacMillan & Co., 1959.

The Elements of Grammar, Margaret Shertzer. New York: MacMillan & Co., 1986.

The Write Way, by Richard Lederer and Richard Dowis, New York: Pocket Books, 1995.

Index

MEET THE AUTHOR

Smoky Trudeau is an author and editor with such passion for the written word she became a workshop instructor in the hopes of passing that passion onto others. She has led her writing and creativity workshops at several Illinois community colleges and other venues across the country.

Graduated from North Central College in Naperville, Illinois, with a degree in psychology, Smoky jokes it took her 17 years to finish her degree because she majored in every subject except physics.

Her diverse interests led to a career as a freelance writer. Her articles have appeared in publications such as *Chicago Parent, Natural Health,* and *First for Women.* Her newspaper column, "Earth Beat," ran in several Illinois newspapers.

Smoky gave up feature writing to turn her attention to fiction and poetry. Her short stories have appeared in literary journals such as *Potpourri* and *CALYX*; poetry in *We'Moon, PanGaia,* and *SageWoman* magazines. Her story, *The Last Flight Home*, was nominated for the 2003 Pushcart Prize. She is the author of two novels, *Redeeming Grace* and *The Cabin.*

She lives in the Midwest but dreams of one day moving to sunny California. The mother of two grown children, when she isn't writing she enjoys organic gardening, reading, and travel.

MORE TERRIFIC BOOKS

BY SMOKY TRUDEAU

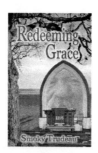

Redeeming Grace

ISBN 978-0-9814739-2-5

The tragic deaths of her mother and two younger siblings have left Grace Harmon responsible for raising her sister Miriam and protecting her from their abusive father, Luther, a zealot preacher with a penchant for speaking in Biblical verse who is on a downward spiral toward insanity.

Otto Singer charms Grace with his gentle courtship and devotion to his brother, Henry. But after their marriage, Otto is unable to share with Grace the terrible secret he has kept more than twenty years. Otto believes he is responsible for a tragic accident that claimed the life of a young woman and left Henry severely brain damaged.

Luther's insane ravings and increasingly violent behavior force Grace to question and reassess the patriarchal religious beliefs of her childhood. Then tragedy strikes just when Otto's secret is uncovered, unleashing demons that threaten to destroy the entire family. Can Grace find the strength to save them, and in the process find her own redemption?

Redeeming Grace is set on Maryland's eastern shore in the late 1920's. The book will appeal to lovers of literary fiction who enjoy theological debate and who understand happy endings, in novels as in life, sometimes come at a heavy price.

The Cabin

ISBN 978-0-9814739-5-6

James-Cyrus Hoffmann has just inherited his grandfather's farm, and with it a mysterious cabin deep in the woods on Hoffmann mountain; a cabin he has dreamed about since childhood. When James-Cyrus enters the cabin, he is vaulted back through time to the Civil War era, where he meets Elizabeth, the brave young woman who lives in the cabin, and Malachi, a runaway slave. James-Cyrus realizes his dreams of the cabin were visions of the past, and that Elizabeth is his great-great aunt—a woman who vanished without a trace from the family tree. He also learns of his ancestors' pivotal role in the lives of dozens of runaway slaves who were offered a safe haven at the cabin, a station on the underground railroad.

Cora Spellmacher, James-Cyrus's elderly friend and neighbor, begins to unravel the secret of how he is able to make his fantastic leaps back and forth through time. In doing so, Cora begins to hope a tragic wrong from her own past can be righted, and that she can regain something precious that was lost to her many years earlier.

The dreams continue, and James-Cyrus realizes Elizabeth and Malachi are in terrible danger. With Cora's help, James-Cyrus undertakes a daring plan of rescue that promises to rewrite his family history and change all of their lives forever.

VANILLA HEART PUBLISHING
BOOK ORDER FORM

2 Easy Ways to Order!

___ copies ***The Cabin*** by Smoky Trudeau $13.95

___ copies ***Redeeming Grace*** by Smoky Trudeau $13.95

___ copies ***Fore-Word, Back-Word, Insight-Out*** $13.95
by Smoky Trudeau

Book Order Total $ _____

Add shipping & handling:

-- $4.00 for U.S. & Canada (up to three books)

-- $10.00 per book for other countries

+ Shipping $ _____

Washington State residents only
  add 8.6% SALES TAX per book   Tax $ _____

TOTAL ENCLOSED $ _____

Mail this form with check or money order to: Vanilla Heart Publishing, 10121 Evergreen Way, 25-156, Everett, WA 98204 and please include shipping information (name, address, etc. and email for confirmation. *Thanks, and Happy Reading!*

OR
Save Even More at

http://shop.vanillaheartbooksandauthors.com/main.sc

Printed in the United States
124902LV00004B/204/P